In Search of Origins

W9-AOX-474

In Search of Origins
The experiences of adopted people

John Triseliotis

Foreword by
Jane Rowe

Routledge & Kegan Paul
London and Boston

First published in 1973
by Routledge & Kegan Paul Ltd
Broadway House, 68-74 Carter Lane,
London EC4V 5EL and
9 Park Street,
Boston, Mass. 02108, U.S.A.
Printed in Great Britain
at the St Ann's Press, Park Road, Altrincham

ISBN 0 7100 7534 0

To Paul and Anna

Contents

Foreword

This is an important book about a small and rather unusual group of adopted people—those who were sufficiently curious about their origins to go to Register House in Edinburgh to see their birth registration. Dr Triseliotis has shown that, if this urgent need for information were typical of adopted persons generally, the number applying to Register House would be very much larger than it is.

The group whose individual experiences are so vividly portrayed in this study was inevitably weighted towards less successful adoptions because, as Dr Triseliotis found, a need to seek original parents was often associated with lack of satisfying relationships within the adoptive family. However, there is evidence both in this country and abroad that adopted people usually are to some extent curious about their origins, and it seems fairly clear that many of them would like more information than is available from their adoptive parents.

In this respect, the adoptees in the study reported here may well have spoken for most adopted persons. They have provided insights into problems of adoption and identity which will be of real value to those who are professionally responsible for the creation and support of adoptive families. Because the experiences of the people in this group were often rather extreme, problems were highlighted and so could be studied more easily. The intensity of their needs, coupled with what was evidently most sympathetic and supportive interviewing, enabled many to express their feelings with a depth and clarity which more happily adopted people would probably not have been able to achieve.

It is one of the many merits of this book that the adoptees have been permitted to speak for themselves. Although the findings have been set into a helpful framework of theory, and Dr Triseliotis has made a number of profoundly important comments and suggestions, he has not allowed his interpretations to come between the reader and the direct source of information. The central part of the book is, in effect, a linked series of quotations from the adoptees who were interviewed. So often, in research, the individual becomes lost in a deluge of statistics. This has not happened here and the result is convincing and vivid.

For many years now social workers and adoptive parents have seen 'telling' as the crux of adoption, not only for its intrinsic importance, but also because it reflects and intensifies other aspects of family relationships. We have learned from other research into the outcome of adoptions that the emotional climate in the home is much more important than material factors. This present work has reinforced these findings, and has shown that the timing and method of revealing adoption were less significant than the parents' capacity to provide over the years a loving and secure environment, which fostered in the child a feeling of confidence and self worth. Because these capacities and characteristics are difficult to identify in childless adoptive applicants, current selection procedures are open to criticism.

Dr Triseliotis also makes some important suggestions for initiating and improving follow-up services for adoptive families and for providing channels for adopted people to obtain essential information about their origins. Many of these recommendations have now been included in the report of the Departmental Committee on the Adoption of Children. In the debates which will no doubt be forthcoming on any new legislation, this book will provide much needed facts and some firm ground for rational discussion of an emotionally loaded subject.

JANE ROWE

Acknowledgments

I should like to take this opportunity to express my deepest thanks and appreciation to a number of people without whose help this study would not have been possible. My warmest thanks go to the seventy adoptees who so patiently and willingly tried to help me to understand some of their personal experiences and feelings as adopted people, in the hope that the information might prove enlightening to adoptees and adoptive parents in general. Many thanks are also due to the Registrar-General for Scotland and particularly to Mr Robertson for their unequalled co-operation in bringing the study to the notice of the adoptees. Similarly my thanks go to the Social Work Services Group (Scotland) for financing the project.

I am equally indebted to Jane Rowe, the Director of the Association of British Adoption Agencies, for her enthusiastic support, suggestions and criticisms, to my wife for making endless corrections to the manuscript and to Mrs Chuter, the Secretary, for her arduous job in spending long hours listening to and typing from the tapes. Finally to Mr David Williams of the Department of Statistics, Edinburgh University, for his statistical advice.

For permission to quote from E. F. Watling's translation of Sophocles, *King Oedipus*, I wish to thank Penguin Books Ltd.

Aims and background

Background to the study

To my knowledge Scotland and Finland are the only countries in the Western world where an adopted person can obtain from official records information that could lead to the tracing of the original parents. Under the provisions of the Adoption Act the Registrar-General maintains an Adopted Children's Register in which entries are made following every adoption order. He also keeps an index of the Adopted Children's Register which is open to public search. In addition the Registrar-General keeps a register which makes traceable the connection between an entry in the register of births which had been marked 'adopted' and any corresponding entry in the Adopted Children's Register. In England such registers are not open to inspection or search 'except under an order of a Court . . .', but the Scottish system provides that information from this register can be made available to the adopted persons themselves after they have attained the age of seventeen.

There is no definite information about the reasons that prompted the Scottish Standing Committee in the House of Commons to insert this section in the Scottish Adoption Act of 1930. No minutes of the Committee's discussion were kept. The only possible explanation is that this would make it possible for the adopted person to claim any inheritance from his biological parents to which he was entitled under the Act. In fact it was not until 1964 that an adopted person in Scotland could inherit from his adoptive parents and that he would have no right to an inheritance from his biological parents. However, a similar situation existed in England until 1949 and yet no such provision was made in the English Adoption Act of 1926. It is improbable that the Scottish Act of 1930 was recognising the importance of identity in its provision for such information to be made available.

Any person over the age of seventeen, who has been adopted in Scotland can now write to or visit Register House in Edinburgh and, on production of evidence about himself, ask for a copy of his original birth certificate. Information that is usually available on such certificates includes the names of the parent(s), the child's original name, its place and date of birth, the occupation of the natural parent(s) and their usual address at the time of the child's birth. In the years 1961 to 1970 an average of forty-two people (or 1·5 per thousand of adopted people over seventeen years old) each year applied to or called at Register House and obtained this information from their original birth certificates. The lowest number of enquiries was fifteen in 1964 and the highest seventy in 1970. Public discussion of adoption usually generates more enquiries as was the case in 1970 when some attention was focused on adoption practice.

The Houghton Committee Report[1] published in October 1970 considered whether the existing right of access to original birth records should be withdrawn, but decided to wait until the results of this study were made available. The committee was concerned about the danger of adopted children tracing their original parents in circumstances where this might not be welcomed by the latter. The committee wished to strengthen anonymity that would help to protect both the child and the adoptive parents on the one hand and the natural parents on the other. Equally the adoptive home and any new family of the natural parents may need protection from interference by the other party or the fear of this.

Aims

The main aim of the study was to identify the general circumstances of adopted adults who seek information about their origins; to establish their reasons for the search, their motivation, their needs and objectives and also to what use they put the information gained. To make such an assessment possible it was important to learn about the adoptees' relevant past and current life situations; about possible internal and external pressures and about the quality of their relationships and their self-perception.

When the project was planned it was hoped that answers to certain questions might not only further understanding of the adoption situation but also point towards desirable areas for legal reform and for practice changes.

Theoretical considerations and related research

The literature on adoption stresses the need for adopted people to learn about their adoption very early on and also to receive as much

2

information as possible about their origins and their background. This, it is claimed, should strengthen the adopted person's sense of identity and contribute to his general well-being. Adoption agencies urge adoptive couples to tell children about their adoption as early as possible and to share relevant information about their background. There has been more controversy as to the exact stage at which adopted children should be told, and also as to whether the adopted person should have access to information that might be used in tracing his biological parent(s). One dissenting voice is that of Ansfield,[2] a psychiatrist, who in a recent publication urges parents not to tell their children that they are adopted to avoid hurting them. Ansfield suggests various devious ways of avoiding telling the child and asks parents to take care not to tell friends and others about the adoption. He concludes that there is no reason to believe that children are better off if they are told that they are adopted.

The how and when of 'telling' are still very controversial questions for which adoption practice and research offer no clear guide-lines. Adoption agencies have for the past thirty to forty years been advising adopting couples to tell the children preferably from the toddler stage. Similarly judges and magistrates who hear adoption applications try to impress on couples the need for telling. The report of the Houghton Committee notes the importance of telling a child that he is adopted and that he needs to know about his origins and adds:

> there is a growing recognition that he [the child] needs to know
> about his origins—about his parents, for instance, the type of
> people they were, their appearance, any special qualities or
> gifts they may have had, their reason for giving him up, any
> special medical features—for the proper development of a sense
> of identity and in order that he and his adoptive parents may
> have a fuller understanding of him as an individual with his
> own unique combination of characteristics both inherited and
> acquired from his upbringing and environment.

The explanation for this advice is that early knowledge by the child of his adoptive status will prevent possible future trauma from finding this out suddenly when older and having to incorporate this important fact into his self-conception. The readiness of adoptive applicants to tell the child about his status is usually an important factor in determining their acceptance as prospective adopters. Such

3

readiness or unreadiness has been linked by some with the adoptive applicants' general sense of security or resolution of feelings about their infertility. Telling the child about his adoption has also been likened to telling him about sex, childbirth, etc. and that the timing of these two aspects is interdependent.

Recently some doubts have been cast on the advisability of telling the child at a very early stage when it is still grappling with some other vital developmental tasks. Schechter,[3] for instance, explained the prevalence of emotional disturbance among adopted children as being due to the timing and period of telling the child that he is adopted when this is done during the period of three to five years, that is when ambivalence is still very strong. Reservations have also been voiced by Peller[4] who comments:

> It is my conviction that adoption should be discussed with the child after his social orbit has widened, after he has met other children and their parents, that is, in his early school years. . . . It seems that in these years a child can learn about his adoption with less upset than earlier and later in his life.

Kirk[5] has also criticised adoption agencies for failing to be sensitive to the dilemma implicit in the apparent social work emphasis upon recommending complete 'candor' with the child about his adoption and about his birth status. He feels that adoption agencies too often err in insisting that adoptive parents tell the child he is adopted without at the same time helping them to anticipate the pangs of pain that are invariably aroused by the awareness that this information is potentially disruptive to the adoptive child and his family.

The readiness of the adoptive parents and their own degree of comfort in deciding when and how to tell the child about his adoptive background is now increasingly stressed. Bernard[6] after considerable experience as a psychiatric consultant to an adoption agency has suggested, regarding this matter, that 'when parents feel comfortable and secure enough of themselves, they do not need to overdo or underdo on this score. They neither force the topic on the child, inopportunely, nor discourage his further questioning by closing the issue after it has been dealt with "once and for all".'

Krugman[7] in discussing the parental task in adoption points out that most adoptive parents come to adoption because of highly personal reasons. It is not yet an unquestioned 'thing to do' as are

4

so many other actions. The thwarting of a couple's desire for parent-hood is deeply personal, and it is often deeply painful. One main task for these parents is to maintain a positive self-image while resolving their own feelings about parenting a child not bound to them by birth. And they have the job, in common with all parents, of helping children to grow and to meet their own problems effectively. The degree to which natural or adoptive parents are able to sustain an adequate image of themselves as people will influence their ability to help their children to develop their own adequate self-image. The unique task of the adopted child, maintains Krugman, is to handle the issues of identity raised by living in a child-parent relationship that originated in social rather than biological acts. Krugman also adds that the child adopted in infancy has no initial pain of a thwarted goal, nor is the question of his entry into adoption related to attempts at mastery of pain during his first or second years. The child, in contrast to his parents, can approach his first awareness of adoption with no direct experience of either pain or loss connected with it, and with nothing in his own experience to suggest that pain, difficulty, or future distress are linked to it.

   One other major developmental problem associated with adopted children is what Freud[8] described as the fantasy of the family romance. Freud described the family romance as a common fantasy of most children in middle childhood, in which they engage when they feel frustrated and threatened by their parents. They resort to the fantasy that the parents with whom they live are not their true parents, but adoptive or step-parents. The idea of another set of 'all-loving, all permissive' parents is comforting, and is said to derive from the child's normal ambivalence of feelings toward his parents. The fantasy represents a brief stage, and is abandoned once the child accepts that he can love and hate the same individual. For an adopted child, however, it is not a fantasy that the parents with whom he lives are not his natural parents; he has, in reality, two sets of parents.

   Schechter[9] and Peller[4] further claim that telling the child during the oedipal period (approximately when three to five years old) heightens the family romance fantasy so that the child idealises his natural parents. Schechter thinks the adopted child may seek the 'good real parents' or, on the other hand, may identify with the 'bad own parents'. In contrast to this is Krugman's[7] point of view. She believes that the young child, on being told of adoption, accepts this knowledge fairly easily. He has not experienced adoption as anything different or painful at this point. Later, as the child seeks more accurate biological information about his ancestry, he moves into the difficult period of resolving his identity for himself. Often the child asks about his biological parents out of intellectual curiosity, and not out of doubts regarding the adequacy of the adoptive parents. Krugman thinks that telling a child of his adoption, and the child's resolution of this identity question, can be ego-strengthening rather than ego-weakening. McWhinnie,[10] in her study of adopted adults, suggests that adoptive parents should inform the child of its adoptive status before the age of five to avoid risk of trauma. Although the foster and adopted children, in her study, could not ask their adoptive parents, they wanted to be given information about their biological parents and the reasons for their placement. Adoptive parents themselves often found it difficult to discuss adoption.

Clothier[11] and Schechter[3] maintain that the correction of the 'family romance' fantasy may be more difficult for an adopted child than for a non-adopted one. Schwartz[12] adds that, in his view, the probability of conflicts in identification with the adoptive parents is likely to be increased for these children, if only because the unknown parental figure may continue to exist as a possible identification model. In extreme cases, the child could continue to focus all positive feelings on the fantasied 'good' natural parents and all the negative feelings on the adoptive parents, resulting in rejection of the values and prohibitions of the adoptive parents.

In contrast to Clothier's[11] and Schecter's[3] interpretations Lawton and Gross[13] believe that if a child is placed in infancy, then logically, he would enhance the image of the adoptive parents in the fantasy and not that of the natural parents, of whom he has had no experience as parents. Kohlsaat and Johnson[14] maintain that prolongation and fixation of the family romance in the adopted child is primarily an expression of the adoptive parents and their role as parents. This position rejects any notion of the family romance as a universal source of problems for the adopted child *per se*, and instead implicates the relative healthiness of family relationships as the major factor for determining the impact of the fantasy in a specific situation. Schwartz[12] concluded from his comparative study that the problems in identification behaviour associated with the special nature of the family romance fantasy were not characteristic of the adoptees in his study and perhaps not in general of children placed in infancy. There was no indication, from his study, that prolongation or fixation of the family romance is a universal characteristic of adopted children. He poses the possibility, however, that the fantasy may have some impact in the lives of other adoptees, for example, children adopted at a relatively older age or children brought up in one or more foster homes.

According to a number of psychiatric studies and observations, the adopted child is also more likely to have emotional and social problems than the non-adopted. Studies by Goodman, Silberstein and Mandell[15], Kirk, Johassohn, and Fish[16], Schecter,[3] Simon and Senturia,[17] Reece and Levin,[18] and Humphrey and Ounsted[19] all report a rather serious degree of disturbance in the adoptive clients coming for psychiatric help. Some of the more carefully designed studies suggest that anything from 3 to 13 per cent of their clients come from adoptive families. Humphrey and Ounsted[19] found from their British study that the proportion of adopted children in their hospital population (2·9 per cent) was more than double. They found a greater tendency to lying, stealing and destructive behaviour in the adoptive group. Simon and Senturia[17] observe that the adopted child, more frequently than the non-adopted one, is diagnosed as manifesting a personality disorder or transient situational personality disorder. In the natural child the predominant diagnoses were neuroses and psychosis. Another interesting finding quoted was that there were fewer referrals of adopted children in the adult range (over twenty-one). The authors believed that since the prevalent disorders in the adopted children are anti-social in nature, the adopted child is not conflicted and does not refer himself in adulthood for help as the more neurotic natural child would. The data from the studies quoted do not reliably support the hypothesis that adopted children are more vulnerable to stress than other children. Such studies have been criticised for their sampling methods and their reliance on clinical populations.

In a follow-up study Jaffe and Fanshel[20] reported the perceptions of a sample of adoptive parents concerning the development and adjustment of their adopted children. The writers discovered, as might have been expected, a wide range of life adjustments among their 100 adoptees. Many had manifested remarkably few problems and were also currently functioning satisfactorily. On the other hand a number of adoptees had experienced a variety of quite serious problems in growing up and some were still contending with major adjustment difficulties at the time their parents were interviewed. Between these extremes was a group whose adjustment over the years and presently could be classified as middle range. The authors agree that they were not in a position to determine whether this incidence of problems was more than one would expect to find among a comparable sample of non-adoptive families, but add that remarkably few of the problems reported were thought to be due to adoption.

Elonen and Schwartz,[21] presenting the conclusions of a follow-up check on a group of children more than a decade after adoption, reported that the adopted children were able to adjust as successfully as non-adopted children. Some adopted children became delinquent, but they were in the minority. The percentage of delinquency was the same as for the non-adopted children. In considering the question of whether the status of an adopted child is a specific factor in the development of particular emotional and social problems, the study found that being adopted is not a causative factor *per se* in the emotional problems of adopted children. The writers go on to add that as with all children, adopted or non-adopted, problems stem from their parents' reactions to them, to their questions and feelings, and to important events in family life.

Comparative studies have been used as the nearest approach to determine the outcome of adopted and non-adopted groups of children. In most of these the emphasis is on the testing of intelligence and personality adjustment supplemented by interviews and school performance. One of the most comprehensive and detailed studies was by Witmer and her associates.[22] They compared a group of 484 adopted children placed independently in Florida, with 484 control children living with their natural parents. Witmer concluded that their large adopted sample showed only slightly poorer adjustment than controls, and that this difference almost disappeared when those adopted after the first month of life were excluded. The children placed at an older age accounted for most of the problem children. The study's over-all conclusion was that adoption outcome was satisfactory or reasonably satisfactory in 80 per cent of the cases. Hoopes and her associates[23] studied a randomly selected sample of 100 adopted children and matched it with a control group of 100 natural children. Their over-all conclusions were that the adopted children did not differ significantly from the natural children in intelligence, or in either the objective or projective personality measures. There was in effect no evidence of greater emotional problems in the sample of adopted children than in the control group. The only significant difference found between the two groups of children was based on teachers' ratings. Like Witmer, the writers add that the child who comes to adoption from a background of emotional deprivation and multiple mothering has greater problems in later adjustment than the child who does not come from such a background. Another of their conclusions was that 'even when problems related to communication about adoption occurred, they did not affect the child's overall functioning'. This finding may be linked, however, with the over-all description of the type of family involved in the study: middle and upper class, soundly educated and economically secure, 'valuing achievement and social co-operation', 'more likely than not to repress or deny hostile, aggressive or other unacceptable feelings and actions'.

In contrast to Witmer's[22] and Hoopes's[23] studies a recent Swedish study makes somewhat different claims. Bohman[24] studied 168 children who were ten to eleven years old at the time of the follow-up. A control group was also obtained in the form of classmates of the same sex and certain comparisons were also made with all their classmates of the same sex. The study found an over-representation of behavioural, but not of social, disturbances among adopted boys and that this was possibly connected with the adoptive situation itself and the disturbances that this involves in the relationship between parents and child. The study's findings relied heavily on teachers' ratings and may have recorded a similar bias to that of Hoopes's.[23] What the studies were possibly recording was the teachers' perception of adopted children as a minority group and of adoption as a state of deprivation bound to have some effect.

If it is the view of adoption agencies that the child should know of his adoption as soon as he can comprehend the concept, the obvious question is whether such knowledge and communication is closely related to success. Neither Brenner[25] nor Lawder[26] in their studies found a clear relationship between ease of communication with the child about his adoption and outcome. Jaffe and Fanshel[20] claimed that there was little correlation between the adjustment of the adopted persons and how and when they learned about their adoption. They discovered that the way parents dealt with the revelation of adoption was by and large a reflection of a more basic underlying orientation to child rearing in general. Families which tended to take a sheltering approach to the general upbringing of their children were also likely to underplay the adoptive status of their children. They tended to postpone revelation, to give minimal information about the child's biological background, to decrease the visibility of the adoptive status and, in effect, to simulate a biological parent-child relationship. On the other hand, parents with a less protective orientation toward the rearing of children were likely also to be more 'open' about adoption and to reveal more information about the natural parents. Only 12 per cent of the parents, in their sample, had shared with their children the true facts of adoption as they knew them. Adoptees who showed marked curiosity about their biological past and desired to learn more about it than their adoptive parents knew or were willing to divulge tended to manifest a more problematic adjustment. None of the other aspects of the 'telling' or the timing of initial revelation, the nature and amount of material revealed, or the frequency of subsequent reference to adoption was appreciably correlated with outcome.

With the exception of McWhinnie's[10] work, there is no other comprehensive study which relies on eliciting information from adopted adults. Most of McWhinnie's sample had been adopted during World War I and many of the adoptive parents failed to inform the children about adoption, the latter finding out mostly from outside. In Sweden recognition of the need to tell a child about its adoption as early as possible is a comparatively recent development. Yet Bohman[24] reports a very high percentage of children who were told before the age of five (68 per cent). Practically all those who had not told the child experienced this as a problem. In a recent study from Czechoslovakia, Vodak *et al.*[27] found that the majority of adoptive parents 'refuse to tell the child that he (she) is not their own'. On the other hand, in Witmer's study of children who were adopted independently in Florida at the time of World War II, as many as 90 per cent of the adoptive parents had explained the relationship to the child.

Because this group of adoptees had not previously been studied it was difficult at the outset to be precise about the type of information obtainable. After the first few interviews it was made evident, however, that they wanted to talk about their relationships, their self-perception and the meaning of their adoption situation to the present search. Almost every one of them viewed his situation and experience as special and hoped that the sharing of it would help others.

The sample

The eventual sample was made up of seventy adoptees who applied or called at Register House in Edinburgh asking to be supplied with information from their original birth entries. An ongoing study was set up with the co-operation of the Registrar-General, who agreed to forward or hand to every enquirer a copy of our letter telling them about the study and asking for their help. It was left to the adoptees to get in touch with the writer if they wished to participate. The ongoing study covered the period 1 December 1969 to 30 November 1970. As it was thought that a year's sample might not be numerically satisfactory and because of the need to understand to what use the adoptees put the information, it was decided to approach also those who had enquired in the last twelve months prior to the commencement of the ongoing study. However, because prior to the commencement of the study the Registrar-General did not keep a record of the addresses of people who called but only of those who wrote, contact could be established only with some of this earlier group.

During the period of the ongoing study 73 adoptees (36 male and the rest female) wrote or called for information, 50 (20 male and 30 female) responded and were interviewed. Of a total of 42 persons (21 male and 21 female) who had written in the year prior to the commencement of the study, 20 (9 male and 11 female) were interviewed. In all, of a possible 98 adoptees (47 male and 51 female), the study interviewed 70 (29 male and 41 female). Considering the very personal nature of the study this must be a very satisfactory response. The good response was solely due to the desire of most adoptees to share experiences that might be of some benefit alike to other adoptees and to adoptive parents. The response was greater from female than male adoptees and it may indicate a different attitude between the sexes towards being interviewed on topics of a personal nature. At least five adoptees who wanted to participate in the study could not be included either because they were abroad or because no mutually convenient time could be found for the interviews.

1970 was a year when considerable publicity was given to adoption practice because of the deliberations of the Houghton Committee. Fortunately for us, this happened when the study was almost at an end, so avoiding the possibility of a rather artificial interest which could have altered the nature of the study. Only two adoptees in the sample appeared to have been motivated by this publicity and the strength of their motivation as well as their expectations and experiences differed from the rest. The study assumes considerable significance because of the finding that eight out of ten adoptees had no knowledge that such information could be given to them as a 'special' right provided in the Adoption Act. They thought that every citizen was entitled to his original birth certificate and they called or wrote for it. They were greatly surprised to hear that, had they been adopted in England or in many other countries, they would not be able to obtain such information. The assumption, therefore, is that if more adopted people felt the need for information from their original birth certificates they would simply have written or called at Register House for it.

Methodology

For the collection of the material the study relied on the non-directive interview. The interviews were conducted by the writer and they lasted from one and a half to two and a half hours. In many instances second interviews were arranged. Most of the discussions were tape-recorded and detailed notes were kept for the rest.

The quality of the interviewing is very important in this kind of study. It is not enough for the interviewer to be 'sensitive' or 'kind' or 'a good listener'. It also demands considerable knowledge of the subject matter to be able to respond, comment or divert appropriately. Whilst it is important to go at the person's pace, it is equally necessary to make connections in response to the respondent's remarks thus making it possible for him to participate fully and avoid a stilted question-and-answer process. By responding to each person's readiness and area of interest it was possible to establish a rapport with the adoptees which permitted the interviewer to enter their kind of thinking, their perceptions and experiences.

Some characteristics of the adoptees

Eight of the adoptees (or 11 per cent) had been adopted within their families and the rest by non-relatives. The percentage of persons, who were adopted by relatives and who were now searching into their background, appears small when compared with the approximately 30 per cent that are adopted each year within their families.

Age at search

At the time of the search one in every ten adoptees was under twenty years old, and approximately one in every seven was forty and over (see Table 1). The earlier assumption that most of the enquirers would be teenagers, taking advantage of this opportunity when they reached the age of seventeen, was not true. The age-group of twenty-five to twenty-nine accounted for almost one-third of the enquirers. It is important to note here that the adoption of three out of five adoptees took place in the 1940s and early 1950s when adoptive parents were strongly advised to tell the children of their adoption.

Table 1   *Age at search (n=70)*

	Age group					
	Under 20	*20–24*	*25–29*	*30–34*	*35–39*	*40 and over*
n	7	14	22	12	5	10
%	10	20	32	17	7	14

Age at placement

Age of adoptees at placement

Well over one-fifth of the adoptees were placed in their adoptive homes when a year or older (see Appendix: Table 2.1). Three out of every five were placed when six months or younger.

Material and methods

Age of adoptive parents at placement

The adoptees' parents were considerably older at placement compared with adoptions taking place in, for instance, 1965.[1] This, however, could represent the pattern of adoptions at the time the adoptees' placements occurred (see Appendix: Table 2.2).

Educational and occupational background

Three out of every five adoptees had left school at the statutory school-leaving age. Just under one-fifth attended beyond the usual school-leaving age and another fifth attended or were still attending college or university. Though a small proportion said they experienced pressures from their parents to achieve academic success, an equal number said that they were not encouraged enough.

The adoptees in the sample were representative of all occupational groups (see Table 2). Even allowing for the fact that the nature of occupations changes from generation to generation, the adoptees in the sample did as well as, and in some instances better than, their adoptive parents, and certainly better than the average in the population.

Table 2 *Occupation background (n=70)**

	Professional, technical and managerial	*Skilled (non-manual)*	*Skilled (manual)*	*Semi-skilled and unskilled*	*Not employed*
	n	*n*	*n*	*n*	*n*
Adoptees	22	8	26	14	
%	31	12	37	20	
Adoptive parents	21	6	22	19	2
%	30	9	31	27	3

* Married women are classified by their husband's occupation

Family composition

Four of the adoptees in the sample were adopted by single women. Twenty-two adoptees were brought up in a single or one parent family by the age of sixteen either because of parental death, separation or

14

adoption by a single person. Just over half of the adoptees were brought up as only children (see Table 3). The rest were adopted in homes where there were already children or where children were born or adopted subsequently, or both. The percentage of only children in the sample was similar to that found in adoptions taking place in 1965.[1] This suggests that those enquiring into their origins represent equally only children and children brought up with siblings.

Table 3   *Siblings in the adoptees' families (n=70)*

	None	Older	Younger	Both older and younger
n	37	15	13	5
%	53	21	19	7

The adoptees' goals

The adoptees who took the step to find out about their origins did so mostly after considerable thought and hesitation. The seventy featuring in the study embarked on their enquiries with the following goals in mind:

(a) Forty-two adoptees (or 60 per cent) had as their main goal the finding of their natural parents. (This group will be referred to as the *Meet the Natural Parents group*)

(b) Twenty-six adoptees (or 37 per cent) were mostly interested in obtaining information about their sociological and biological origins and not in meeting their natural parents. (This group will be referred to as *Background Information group*)

(c) The remaining two adoptees were searching for their original birth entries with a very practical goal in mind. The first was asked to produce certain information before he could get security clearance for a Civil Service job and the second needed the information for a wedding that was to take place outside Britain. (Because of the rather special circumstances of these two adoptees they were excluded from the rest of the sample.)

Of the 42 adoptees who were interested in meeting their original parents, three out of every five were searching for their mothers. Of the remaining 17, two were interested in their fathers only, whilst the remaining 15 were keen to meet both the natural parents. Of the 26 adoptees who wished to have more background information, six were predominantly interested in information about their natural mother and her genealogy, four were exclusively interested in their father's genealogy and the remaining 17 were curious to find out about both their birth parents. Significantly fewer adoptees in the Meet the Natural Parents group were interested in both parents than in the Background Information group. It was the adoptees' hope that the attainment of their respective goals would eventually lead to greater 'happiness', 'satisfaction' or 'adjustment'.

In the absence of a properly controlled group, it is difficult to say how far the adoptees who set out each year in search of their origins are similar to or different from those who never take such a step. Using McWhinnie's[2] sample which was drawn from the general adopted adult population in one part of South East Scotland, certain similarities and differences can be seen with regard to a number of sociological characteristics. Most of our sample was adopted considerably later than McWhinnie's and was somewhat younger at the time of the interview. A greater number was also classified in social classes I and II, compared with McWhinnie's. The adoptees in McWhinnie's study were placed for adoption at a slightly younger age but more were placed with adoptive mothers aged forty and over. A higher percentage of adoptees in our sample found out about their adoption when aged sixteen and over.

The study focuses considerably on the two groups of adoptees that were identified, i.e., the Meet the Natural Parents group and the Background Information group. As the two groups show some distinct differences, the study focuses on the circumstances and attitudes responsible for the adoptees' search for their natural parents or background information respectively. This classification in terms of goals was made easy because of the adoptees' clarity and certainty about their objectives.

Early on in each interview the adoptees would usually make clear what their aim was. They would then go on to say what motivated them for the search and what their ultimate expectations were. Though the strength of the adoptees' motivation towards the attainment of their goal varied, by and large they were either seeking their original parents or they were searching for information into their genealogy.

The sequence in this book starts with the revelation of adoption and proceeds to the perception of relationships and of the self; motivation for the search; ultimate expectations; outcome and views. The adoptees' comments are reproduced extensively without alteration. In a number of instances we have consolidated certain passages made at different stages during the interview, to give a more complete and coherent picture of the adoptees' feelings and views. Names, occupations and other identifiable characteristics have been changed to make recognition of individuals impossible. The word 'parent' is used throughout to mean the adoptive parents unless otherwise stated

3   The revelation of adoption

My father was a Corinthian, Polybus;
My mother a Dorian, Merope. At home
I rose to be a person of some pre-eminence;
Until a strange thing happened—a curious thing—
Though perhaps I took it to heart more than it deserved.
One day at table, a fellow who had been drinking deeply
Made bold to say I was not my father's son.
That hurt me; but for the time I suffered in silence
As well as I could. Next day I approached my parents
And asked them to tell me the truth. They were bitterly angry
And I was relieved. Yet somehow the smart remained;
And a thing like that soon passes from hand to hand.
So, without my parents' knowledge, I went to Pytho;
But came back disappointed of any answer
To the question I asked, having heard instead a tale
Of horror and misery; how I must marry my mother,
And become the parent of a misbegotten brood,
An offence to all mankind—and kill my father.
At this I fled away, putting the stars
Between me and Corinth, never to see home again,
That no such horror should ever come to pass.

From Sophocles, *King Oedipus*
(Penguin Books, 1947)

This extract from Sophocles' play *King Oedipus* exemplifies the genealogical bewilderment of most adoptees in the study. The tragedy of Oedipus began when his parents not only failed to reveal his adoptive status to him but also, when he faced them with the possibility, denied it. Oedipus' misfortune is also the misfortune of many adoptees who, taunted by others that they are not the children of their parents, turn to the latter for the truth and then are sometimes deceived. Uncertainty and confusion resulting from ignorance about one's exact origins appears to stimulate pressures of such proportions, that the desire to know or find out becomes difficult to control. The Oedipus story implies that the child who has no knowledge of his natural parents or only uncertain knowledge about them may become genealogically bewildered. The resulting state of confusion and uncertainty may undermine his sense of belonging and identity.

Advice on how best to tell the child that he is adopted varies. There is no neat formula and some suggest a fairy story approach or the 'chosen' story, whilst others advise on revealing the facts as near to the truth as possible.

Age of adoption revelation

The timing of the adoption revelation was based solely on the adoptees' own account. It is therefore possible that some adoptees may have been told earlier about their adoption but obliterated it from their memories. The circumstances described suggested, however, consistent evasiveness and secrecy on the part of many parents.

Almost two out of every three adoptees came to know of their adoptive status when eleven or more years old (see Appendix: Table 3.1). Well over half of them in fact learnt about their adoption when they were sixteen or over. Once telling was left beyond the age of ten the greatest probability was that the child would find out from sources outside his family. In four cases the adoptees came to find out or were told when thirty-five years old and over. Only one out of every six adoptees was told when aged between three and five, the age generally recommended by agencies, courts and by the adoption literature. It is a matter of conjecture whether the high percentage (84 per cent) of adoptees who were told or found out when six years or older is characteristic of the general adopted population or only of this sample. If the latter were true, it would indicate that most of those searching into their genealogical background were people who were told or found out about their adoption at a comparatively late stage. Of forty-four who were told or found out after the age of ten, two out of every three were now trying to meet their natural parent(s) (see Appendix: Table 3.2). It should be acknowledged, however, that half of those who came to know before the age of eleven were also looking for their original parents. These findings, as well as the varied reaction of adoptees to the stress of late revelation, point to the fact that the timing of telling is not of paramount importance and that other factors need to be considered.

The stage of revelation was not found to be related to the social class background of the adoptive parents. The assumption that late revelation would be associated with working-class background and early revelation with middle-class background was not substantiated. The children of a banker, a scientist, two teachers, an engineer and a vicar learnt about their adoptive status at the respective ages of 24, 20, 18, 9, 10 and 4.

Adoptees who were told by their parents when ten years old or younger were significantly more satisfied than those who were told when over the age of ten. All the former adoptees, with the exception of those in whose case the disclosure of adoption took a punitive form, said that the stage of revelation and the way they were told gave them, at the time, a feeling of well-being. No shock or upset was experienced. There was a close association between earlier telling and satisfaction and later telling and extreme dissatisfaction. Those told at around the age of four to eight expressed the greatest satisfaction. In contrast to adoptees who came to know about their adoption when over the age of about ten, the former group did not experience the adoption revelation as distressful or painful. It made some impression on them at the time, but its significance and meaning were more gradual. A real grasp of adoption did not, as a rule, emerge before puberty and adolescence. Where 'telling' was done in a hostile and retaliatory way it left the child with the feeling that it was something 'shameful' or 'terrible'. Similar feelings began to develop also in those whose parents treated the subject with extreme secrecy and evasiveness.

Adoptees who were told or found out when over the age of about ten felt this deeply and it had a profound adverse effect on them. Revelation at this late stage had a stunning effect, shaking their entire life and self-image, leaving most of them confused and bewildered. They felt the need to reassess their whole life and to start 're-discovering' themselves. The later they were told, the greater the distress and confusion. Adoptees in this group made such remarks as 'I was stunned' or 'shocked' or 'numb'; or, 'suddenly I felt that me wasn't me' or, 'I felt it deeply within me'; 'my first thought was who am I then?' or, 'I felt I was nobody', 'I felt I didn't belong' or, 'I was shattered and bewildered.' Subsequently they became intensely preoccupied with questions about their forebears, wanting to find them or to know more about them. The revelation shook their whole being and appeared to upset both the physical as well as the mental image of themselves.

The initial reaction on finding out in adolescence and adult life was one of shock and numbness followed later by intense anger towards their parents, and occasionally towards their original ones. The impact of revelation was so strong that many found it difficult to express emotions about it and simply felt 'lost', 'speechless', 'numb' or 'shattered'. There was some tendency during the first days after revelation to deny the fact and pretend that it was not true. Their reaction to finding out was reminiscent of that of bereaved people who do not want to believe the death of a loved person. Acceptance of the fact of adoption so suddenly and without preparation was beyond their coping capacity.

The initial reaction of shock and speechlessness was followed in a few days by intense anger towards the adoptive parents for withholding information from them. There was criticism and bitterness towards the parents and other small grievances and parental 'failures' were now resurrected. The adoptive mother came in for most criticism, adoptees placing the responsibility for telling on her. Similar bitterness was also directed by some towards the natural mother for giving them up. This was a stage of intense preoccupation with their adoptive status and their first set of parents, especially the mother. They tried to direct their thoughts to their original parents picturing them in different situations, but because they had very little information about them they found this very difficult. Hence an intense wish to find out more: 'You had nothing real to go on' remarked one of them. They implied that their attempts to recapture their 'lost' parents were frustrated because they knew nothing about them. For similar reasons they could not complete the mourning process.

One question that is difficult to answer is how far the considerable confusion and bewilderment that followed the disclosure was because of the great impact and seriousness of the stress itself or because many of these adoptees were already insecure and uncertain about themselves and the revelation simply worsened their situation. Dynamic psychology would maintain that a child who receives good enough care in the early stages of development and goes through them unhampered by serious adverse experiences should, by the completion of the adolescent phase, have established a stable concept of self, feel fairly secure, be certain about his status in the

C

21

group, about his ability to give and take love and have no undue anxieties about how he compares with others. The adult adoptees in the sample who learned late about their adoption were brought up in ignorance of having another set of parents and their whole concept of themselves was based on an identification with their adoptive parents. It meant that following revelation they had to re-define themselves on the basis of only a social and emotional relationship with their adoptive parents rather than a biological one. After the initial shock, some were able to cope with the new situation, but many others seemed to be set back greatly. The evidence showed that the adoptees who coped more successfully with the stress of late revelation had already established a fairly stable self-image based on the adoptive parents as real parents. Those who were entirely shattered and became very distressed and preoccupied with their forebears had already been precariously balanced with a history of an unsatisfactory home life and with difficulties in coping with life situations. In saying this, one should not underestimate the traumatic effect of such a big stress as late revelation of the adoptive status. It is relevant to quote Guntrip[1] here who wrote: 'We have to recognise that individuality and ego-identity, however strongly achieved are always precariously held against threats from the external world.'

Of forty-four adoptees who came to know of their adoption when over the age of ten, two out of every three were now searching for their parents and only one was after background information. It should be acknowledged, however, that half of those who came to know before the age of eleven were also looking for their original parents (see Appendix: Table 3.2). These findings, as well as the varied reaction of adoptees to the stress of late revelation, point to the fact that the timing of telling is not of paramount importance and that other factors need to be considered.

The source of revelation

Well over half the adoptees learnt about their adoption from sources other than their parents (see Appendix: Table 3.1). These sources were mostly other children or documents to which the adoptees had accidental access. There were many instances when the adoptees—not unlike Oedipus—having been told by another child, asked their parents for the truth but the latter vehemently denied it. In spite of parental denials, adoptees were usually left with the nagging feeling that something was wrong and a beginning mistrust of their parents. In some cases adoptive parents, anxious to conceal the adoption, presented their children with short birth certificates which did not record the fact of adoption. It was often years before the adoptees realised that these were only shortened versions of a fuller certificate, and they were then critical of their parents' apparent deception.

Where the adoption was disclosed by the parents it was usually the adoptive mother who revealed the fact. Fathers rarely featured and most adoptees—male and female—did not expect them to take or share this responsibility. Where there was failure to disclose the fact, adoptees were critical of both parents but especially of the mother: 'It was my mother's responsibility to tell me; she should have taken me aside and talked to me . . .'; or 'the mother is the head of the family . . .'; or 'my mother shouldn't have kept it from me'. The focusing of such expectations on the adoptive mother appeared to be a reflection partly of some fathers' attitude that adoption was the sole responsibility of the wife and partly of the adoptees' view that the mother was responsible for all matters within the home and the father for affairs outside.

The association of the adoption revelation with other unhappy experiences was not uncommon among adoptees in the sample. The mother of a girl of twelve committed suicide the day after she talked to her about her adoption. To the girl's utter dismay the father also died a year later and she was now still feeling desolate. In the case of a thirteen-year-old, the father died two days after the revelation of adoption and the mother's re-marriage a year later was experienced as total 'rejection'. The first time a boy of eleven heard of his adoption was when his mother, in a fit of anger, called him an 'adopted rat'. Similar epithets were exchanged in subsequent years. Another adoptee described the revelation as follows:

> I was seven at the time and my mother who was in a very bad
> mood said she would send me back to my 'slut mother'. I
> didn't know what she was talking about, but after that,
> exchanges of this kind were frequent and I realised that my
> mother wasn't my mother, if you know what I mean. Yet I
> I wouldn't dare to ask her who my real mother was.

A girl of sixteen had an argument with her mother on the day she was taking her 'A' level exams and her father, who had deserted the family on a number of occasions, revealed the adoptive situation for the first time by saying, 'You never got on well with us because you are adopted. I was never in favour of it.' Other examples were quoted by adoptees to show that some parents made them feel they regretted having them: 'When the only people you have come to know as parents say this, then you have nowhere to turn. If they feel like this, your relatives by adoption cannot be of any help and you feel alone.'

Adoption never acknowledged

Nine adoptees who found out about their adoption, either through documents or from outside persons, never acknowledged the fact with their adoptive parents. In most of these cases the adoptive parents died with no reference having been made at all to the adoption situation. The adoptees themselves refrained from confronting their parents with the fact, saying, 'If they wanted to tell me they would have done so, no need for me to ask, it was up to them.' A young man of twenty-one came across his adoption certificate when he was twelve. He had told nobody about it through all these years and he was now afraid of taking the initiative for fear of upsetting his parents. It had been a great burden for him, to know without being able to share it. The writer was the first person he ever talked to about his adoption and at the end he remarked, 'Perhaps I can now talk to my mother about it.' Mr Erickson, now a married man, found out about his adoption when he first went to register at the Labour Exchange when he was fifteen. When he opened the sealed envelope, given him by his mother, he found the birth certificate marked with the words 'adopted'. At first he thought it was a mistake and he asked for the help of one of the officials who confirmed the fact:

> I didn't give it much thought at the time and it was some time later that it began to hit me what it was . . . I felt despondent and yet I couldn't go and ask my mother; I still cannot. It is my feeling that she would have told me if she wanted to. I tend to think now that she knows that I know . . . But to me finding this out was a kind of a let-down. When you leave school you're dying to get somewhere, dying to do something new, you are desperate to get out into the world, so to speak, and this knowledge was quite a setback to me. Maybe if I'd found out

earlier it wouldn't have mattered so much; I don't know. It is
difficult to say . . . but I often wished that my parents could
have trusted me and told me. It hits you very hard when you
think of it. At first I became confused and spent long hours
feeling sorry for myself and thinking about my first parents.
There were times when I felt very angry towards my parents for
keeping it from me. But then I said to myself—it must be very
difficult for a woman to suddenly turn round and say—'you are
not mine, like, you are adopted.'

In a more tragic case, when the adoptive mother of a fourteen-
year-old boy died, he read her age on the coffin and for the first time
he worked out that she could not possibly have been his mother
as she was sixty-six at the time of her death. The mother had been
the only surviving parent, there were no other relatives at hand and
he felt at a loss, confirmation of his adoption came later through
the solicitors who were looking after the estate. Mr Tait found out
accidentally when he was fourteen. His mother had died and his
father asked him to find the marriage certificate which was needed
to register the death. Whilst searching for it, he came across his
adoption certificate for the first time. He was greatly shaken to read
it: 'My shock was so great that I can't put it into words. I was
stunned . . . Yet I couldn't go to my father and ask him. I didn't
want to upset him. Three months later he died too and there was
nobody to ask'.

Mr Stanton, who also found out accidentally at the age of twelve
but had not been told by his parents, was not particularly upset or
critical of his parents:

It didn't make any difference—nothing seemed any different
from what it was before I knew. It didn't make any difference
at the time and it still doesn't. I have not mentioned it to my
parents. My father is dead now and my mother may feel it would
turn me against her if she told me. She may also think that it
might make me feel strange with people who are supposed to be
aunts, uncles and cousins . . . she obviously has her own
reasons for not wanting to tell me and I think in a case like this,
it is only right that I should let her have her way. Besides,
how do I go home and say that I found this certificate years
ago and then try to talk about it . . . It is a very difficult thing
to do.

25

The actual revelation and the adoptees' reaction

As stated earlier, almost nine out of every ten adoptees found out or were told about their adoption when aged six years and over. Because of this, most of them had very vivid memories of how this happened.

Revelation by outside sources

Finding out about their adoption from outside sources was experienced as negative and unhelpful by all adoptees in this group. The most frequent outside source was other children or documents that adoptees came across accidentally. In fact in a few cases, the parents moved away from the area for fear that neighbours might tell the adoptee: 'My mother moved house when she adopted me so nobody knew in the new area. But I was told by a girl when I was fourteen. She said she was not allowed to play with me because I was adopted.' In some cases the revelation came from other children often in the form of an attack or vindictiveness. Adoptees mainly reacted by going to their mothers and asking them to tell them whether this was true or not. Whilst some mothers took the opportunity to acknowledge it, others denied it:

> I went home in tears and told my mother that Janet had said they were not my mother and father. My mother then became furious and went to Janet's home and created a real scene. She denied it emphatically and told me how and where she gave birth to me and what a difficult birth it was too . . . But I realised later that it was not my feelings she was concerned about. She was angry because somebody took the liberty to discuss her business . . . It was a year later that my married sister took me aside and told me. I never talked about this with my mother again and she is now dead.

The wife of a coal miner clarified her adoptive status only four years ago when she was seventeen and going through a very turbulent and unhappy adolescence:

> I had a row with Ann—another child. I must have been nine or ten at the time and she told me bluntly that I was adopted and that her mother had asked her not to play with me. I went home and asked my mother who denied it and asked me to stop being

silly. After this, other children would say 'that's not your mother'. I would keep going to my mother and to my godmother who kept saying it was not true. It was only when I got engaged and my fiancé asked my father that the truth came out.

A number of parents, when asked by their children, acknowledged the fact but refused to say anything more at the time or later on: 'After my mother admitted it she refused to say anything more.' Other parents told their children that the reason they did not tell them earlier was because they did not want to hurt them. They genuinely thought that they were protecting them from a painful experience. Yet almost all the adoptees were clear in their own minds that they did not like protection based on 'falsehoods' or 'dishonesty'. Their parents would have stood higher in their estimation if they had been honest with them.

Some adoptees, on finding out from outside sources, were reluctant to ask their parents for fear of upsetting them or for fear that 'it might be true'.

I was thirteen when I was told bluntly by another girl. I was left numb and speechless. The strain was terrible . . . I had headaches and fainting spells and the doctor kept prescribing phenobarbitones for me. My mother told me three years later. She said she always wanted to tell me but did not know how. She was then cross with me that I knew and had kept it to myself; I thought this was very unfair.

In at least five cases the revelation was made by the parents to the adoptees' husband or wife but it was years later that the latter felt able to share it. Husbands or wives in this case perceived adoption as an unpalatable fact that had to be concealed to avoid upsetting the adoptee. Mrs Truman was told by her husband two years after they married but it was another seven years before she could confront her mother with it:

I was shocked when my husband told me. I was twenty then and I was beginning to suspect something fishy going on . . . it was a terrible burden for my mother to put on him. He more or less promised her not to tell me, as he too believed that it was not nice to know that you are adopted. I was just lost when he told me and I didn't know anybody I could go to except my

adoptive mother, but she hadn't told me and so she couldn't
be of any comfort . . . Knowing my mother, the longer she
didn't tell me the worse it was and she just couldn't—in fact,
I truthfully believe that at times she got to the stage she
imagined it didn't happen. But I was shattered at the time as if
a bomb had dropped and I just had the feeling that everything
that I had thought I was, suddenly was stripped away and I
felt bare and I had no idea who I was. I cried for days and
thought a lot about my first mother. I thought of her all the
time. Yet you do not know what she is like or where she is.
Later the whole thing made me turn against my adopted
mother. But I do not feel as bitter now. . . .

Just under one-third of the adoptees in the study came to know
about their adoptive status mainly from documents such as birth
certificates or letters that they came across. Some found out about it
when they went to register at the Labour Exchange or applied for a
passport or were joining the army and had to produce full birth
certificates. 'After the initial shock,' said one of them, 'I resented
my parents for quite some time and my mind was preoccupied with
my birth-mother. I felt then that I was going home to a home where
I didn't really belong.'

Another adoptee, Mrs McSweeny, was about to marry and was
asked to produce a full birth certificate. She had a shortened one and
was unaware at the time that there was any other type. The first she
heard about being adopted was from the Registrar-General's office:

This was a shattering experience and a terrible shock. The way
I found out and when I found out couldn't have been worse.
The timing was disastrous. It must be very difficult for adoptive
parents to find the right moment to tell and if you miss the
right moment you don't know when another one is; years
perhaps; you keep putting it off and rationalising it to
yourself . . . but I think it is wrong; it is like the facts of life;
as soon as the opportunity arises you should take it. It always
feels much worse than it really is but once you get started it is
not so bad . . . Somehow I always felt that I didn't belong and
this crowned it.

Mrs Drummond found out in a different way. She was nineteen
at the time and she was visiting her grandmother who was ill. Whilst

there she was asked to read a letter the grandmother received from a relative. At the end of the letter the writer asked, 'And how is Fiona, the little girl that my sister adopted?' The adoptee was terribly shocked but could not ask her grandmother. She went home to her father, who said it was all 'rubbish'. Next day he was taken ill and was rushed to hospital where he died a few days later. Just before his death the mother acknowledged the fact of adoption but has refused to talk about it ever since. Mrs Drummond felt that if she were told earlier she might not have experienced the revelation so crushingly and might not have felt so bitter about the lack of trust.

Revelation by adoptive parents

In thirty cases (or 44 per cent) the revelation of the adoptive status was made by the parents themselves under diverse circumstances. It was noted above that the earlier the adoptees were told the greater their satisfaction and the later they were told the greater their dissatisfaction. Depending on the stage and the way they were told, adoptees perceived it as either negative or positive.

Of the adoptees who were told by their parents, almost half experienced it as negative and traumatic or as unfortunate, either because of the way or because of the age at which they were told.

Forms of parental 'telling' perceived as negative Adoptees perceived 'telling' as negative in those cases where the parents left it either very late to tell or told them in a hostile way or made belittling references to the adoptees' original background. A young student-teacher was told at five, which she thought was the 'right time' for her, but her parents painted a very black picture of her birth-mother making reference to 'bad blood' and 'bad background' and though she was made to feel very grateful for being adopted she was also resentful. Others described how 'telling' was done in anger accompanied by some malicious reference to the child's illegitimacy or to the original mother's morals. The adoptees implied that the hostility that accompanied 'telling' and the devaluing of the natural mother were not isolated examples but one aspect of a generally negative attitude towards them. These descriptions were made by few adoptees only and the impression formed was of adoptive mothers who were themselves very unhappy using the adoptee as a scapegoat.

Mrs Marshall was coming up to twenty-one and she needed her birth certificate to arrange her wedding. She asked her mother for her birth certificate but the latter insisted on making all the arrangements herself. At the adoptee's insistence the mother became angry and vindictive:

> She told me that I was a bastard and that I was born in the poor house. If I wanted my birth lines I could go and enquire there . . . A few days after this my brother James came to me sobbing and saying that he was only 'an adopted bairn'. [Somebody had told him at the pub that he was illegitimate and adopted.] So I told him that I was adopted too . . . we felt we had no one to turn to. We couldn't talk to our mother and we both cried in each other's arms.

Mr Duncan had been nineteen when he decided to leave home in Scotland and go to work in London. He felt he had to break away from his mother who was too protective and demanding. At the news of his leaving home she became very upset and told him that he was adopted:

> My reaction to it was very violent and I felt utterly confused for days. It also made me feel ungrateful and bad for leaving home . . . I wish I had been told earlier when I could understand it much better . . . My mother being so reticent in telling me perhaps gave me an inborn feeling that it is something you don't want everybody to know . . . that it is wrong. Because of this I did not tell my wife for a long time after we married. I still cannot bring myself to tell my children. When a child understands a little about life, that is the time to tell him.

Mr Colvin, now in his late twenties, said:

> Since the age of ten I knew it within myself that I was adopted. It was an intuition. When I was about to marry I was asked to produce a full certificate and I went to my mother. She was very upset and cross and then told me that I was adopted and that if I wanted to know more I would find some very nasty things about my first parents. I imagined then that my real parents were insane or criminal. There was no one I could turn to and ask and of course I could not ask my father or mother.

Mr Barron always knew that his younger brothers were adopted, though they were not aware of it. He never suspected that he might have been adopted, too, until two years ago when he was thirty-nine. His mother was ill at the time and whilst he sat talking to her one night it came out:

> She thought I knew—although she had never told me—she thought I must have suspected it . . . I just felt it wasn't true. The first time I was told I just couldn't believe it. I couldn't take it in . . .. I was confused . . . I didn't ask her anything more as I did not want to hurt her . . . She died soon after and I never asked her how she came to adopt me . . . but it left me very bitter that she could not trust me earlier . . . Yet I knew about my brothers and I did not tell them.

Forms of parental telling perceived as positive Almost half of those who were told by their parents expressed satisfaction with the way it was done and with its timing. Satisfaction, however, about the way adoption was revealed did not necessarily imply general satisfaction about other aspects in the adoptees' relationships with their parents. There were occasions when the adoption revelation was perceived as 'tactful' but relationships then or subsequently were experienced as unsatisfying.

What distinguished adoptees in this group from the rest was that they were generally told at an earlier age and the telling gave them a feeling of 'well-being', of being 'special' and of having something to be 'proud' of. Though the adoptive parents made little reference to the biological ones, they generally conveyed a good image of them. It is true that adoptees who were told around the ages of four to seven did not comprehend at the time what this was all about and what adoption meant. They thought that they were 'different' and somewhat 'special'. Realisation of the meaning of adoption was a more gradual thing. Actual realisation of what adoption meant and what its implications were did not begin for many of them till after the age of ten or eleven. They had some awareness of another mother and father but feelings around this were dormant till the beginning of puberty or adolescence. Some had read stories at school which made reference to adoption and they had connected them with their own situation.

Miss Smith, now aged eighteen, thinks she was told at about the age of four:

I knew I was adopted as far back as I can remember and I am
grateful to my parents for telling me. It didn't mean anything
at the time except that I was different in some way and that this
made me feel good and special. It is only in the last couple of
years that I started taking notice of my adoption and what it
really means. I haven't been getting on well with my parents
during this time and this has made me think a tremendous lot
about my adoption. . . .

An even happier experience was recorded by Mr McTagart whose
current search had to do with some documentation of his origins:

I was told at the age of ten and this was the best age for me.
Mark you, telling about adoption is like talking about sex to
your children. You can turn round to the textbook and say ten
years of age is the best time, but you must treat every child as
an individual. The time is when the child is ready . . . It didn't
make any real difference, but my parents had a tremendous love
and affection for me and therefore nothing could shake this
relationship. I felt this within myself as a youngster, although I
obviously didn't think this way. I just accepted it naturally and
I knew that even though what they were saying was true, their
words of assurance that came along with it were equally true . . .
I was old enough to appreciate it and I think it was just the
right age for me.

Though some parents disclosed the adoptive status in a positive
way, they saw the revelation as an end in itself and not as the
beginning of a process. The failure to see this as the start of an
ongoing process was attributed either to anxieties and insecurities
in the parents or to sheer ignorance and fear of hurting. It was also
noted that telling the child early was not always a sign of strength,
any more than telling late was necessarily a sign of insecurity.

One adoptee could remember being told at about the age of four,
but she could not remember exactly how. She remembers though
going round and telling everybody about it. She felt it was something
nice which made her feel different from others but also 'great'. The
realisation of what adoption meant did not sink in until much later
in a gradual way. Nothing suddenly happened to her. She wished,
however, that the subject of her adoption had not subsequently
become taboo at home.

A young woman could remember being told by her mother at the age of five, but the implications of it did not sink in till about the age of eleven or twelve. She thought the age of five was right for her. She remembers being told she was 'wanted' and 'chosen' and it made her feel 'both different and special' at the time. She did not mind telling other children about it and she implied that she saw other children who were not like her as 'deprived'. Subsequently she found her parents becoming secretive and evasive and her earlier feelings of being 'special' disappearing.

Irrespective of what experts in this field may have to say, adoptees in this group said that stories about being 'selected', 'chosen', 'special', 'precious', 'needed', etc. made them feel 'good inside' or 'proud' or 'pleased' or 'different and special.' Again these adoptees said that it was not just the way 'telling' was done but also series of other attitudes unconnected with 'telling'. If they were disappointed later on, it was because this sense of well-being did not continue. One adoptee was told at a very young age that she was chosen because her mother, though she loved her very much, could not keep her. She found this explanation very satisfying and it made her feel 'proud'. She wished, however, that her parents had not remained so silent after this revelation which made her start wondering about something being wrong. One adoptee who was told the 'chosen' story had a fantasy of being chosen from a row of babies and this made her feel very special. She realised later that there is perhaps little real choice in adoption, but she did not perceive the 'chosen' story as misleading because it was well meant.

Mr Newson was about eight at the time he was told by his mother. He was very 'impressed' by the revelation though he could not grasp the full meaning of what was being told. He was also told that his own parents wanted him but were unable to keep him because of their circumstances. He realised that his real parents were different and that he had another set of parents. He liked the way he was told. and found it very satisfying. He thought this was the right age for him to be told. If it had been left later there would be the danger of learning about it from outside. In fact when a cousin told him at the age of ten, he was glad he could say that he already knew: 'It would have been awful if it was the first time.' Though there was little reference to his adoption there was no evasion if he asked questions: 'I felt no inhibition about asking. I did not feel that if I asked they would feel annoyed or upset.'

The revelation of adoption

Miss Gibbs was ten when a child told her at school that her parents were not her real parents. Because she saw this as just a piece of malice on the part of the other girl she was not particularly upset. When it was repeated to her a few days later she asked her mother who seemed upset and sorry. She said that she and her husband were wondering which was the right time to tell her and somehow they did not know how to go about it: 'They were sorry that I had to learn about it from outside. I was very surprised myself because my parents brought me up to discuss everything with them. After this I respected them a wee bit more for their frankness.'

Adoptees brought up within their families

As stated earlier eight people were adopted by relatives such as aunts, uncles, grandparents or by one parent and a step-parent. The ages at which they were told or found out accidentally were similar to those who had been adopted outside their families. Four adoptees who were adopted by one or both parents and came to know in adolescence that one of their 'parents' was only a step-parent reacted not unlike other adoptees who were told or found out after the age of about eleven. They were upset and had their 'faith' in their parents 'shaken'. After the revelation they became suspicious and seriously doubted whether the other parent was a real parent. The object of their current search was partly to establish the truth or to seek out the remaining parent: 'If I was told a lie once, the rest may be a lie. I cannot trust that my father is my real father; he may be lying again . . . this is why I want to get to the bottom of this.'

Greater confusion was experienced by the wife of a hospital orderly. She lived with her grandparents from birth and came to call them 'mother' and 'father'. Her own mother lived in the same household and the adoptee knew her as 'auntie'. When her original mother married her original father, they took her away from the grandparents and adopted her, because at the time the adoptee was born they were not free to marry. She was seven when she was removed and she still feels bitter and resentful towards her parents for doing this to her. Once she joined her original parents she had to start calling them 'mother' and 'father' and address her grandparents differently instead of 'parents'. Her grandparents' children whom she knew as brothers and sisters now became 'uncles' and 'aunts'. When she found out at the age of eighteen that she was technically adopted by her original parents she started doubting whether they were her original parents. She firmly believed that they were adoptive parents who 'took' her away from her real parents at the age of seven and were now telling her 'fibs' to cover up. She cleared some of this confusion after writing to Register House. When she was removed from her grandparents she felt 'unwanted' and 'rejected' by them and for months would cry herself to sleep. She has not forgotten the experience or forgiven her parents for having done this to her: 'You do not forget . . . it was a terrible thing to do to me . . . it still hurts . . . it is not easy to forgive them.'

The natural parent romance fantasy

A few adoptees, after being told or finding out about their adoption, developed a firm belief that a particular person who had formerly shown them 'kindness' or given them presents or 'persistently' looked at them, was possibly an original parent. They would then maintain that some personality trait or some physical characteristic or a hobby they had was similar to that of the 'fantasied' parent. Mr Thin, now in his forties, was told about his adoption at fourteen. He believed then, and still does, that his natural father was the owner of a big estate not far from their cottage, because the landlord would pass by their house and always smile at him; on one occasion he remembers the stranger speaking to him. As a child he felt 'different' from other children and he attributed his difficulty in making friends to his possible 'aristocratic' blood.

Another adoptee could remember a woman driving up their road in a big car and asking the children she was playing with to show her Lydia Morris. The woman stayed with them for a few minutes and then left. The adoptee is now certain that this woman was her original mother. Mrs Forfar, who found out about her adoption when she was fifteen, remembers receiving presents every Christmas from some unknown friend of the family but these stopped when she was nine. She is now certain that the presents came from her original mother but that the adoptive parents eventually stopped them. Miss Glenn was told about her adoption when about the age of three or four. She subsequently built up a 'huge fantasy' that a titled lady, who used to visit her preparatory school as one of the governors, was her real mother because she would sometimes watch her play. She would boast to the other children that she was adopted and that her 'lady' mother would come and collect her on her twenty-first birthday. She was bitterly disappointed recently when she found out that her original mother was a domestic help.

Where there was excessive fantasying or idealisation of the original parents, it persisted into adult life. It was mainly a characteristic of adoptees labouring under considerable stress. The fantasying or idealisation provided its own satisfactions for a time and, when this was no longer so, then more concrete steps had to be taken to trace the natural parents.

Conclusions

The majority of the adoptees in the study were told or found out about their adoption well after the age usually recommended by most experts in the field of adoption. The adoptees were overwhelmingly in favour of being told by their own parents and preferably before the age of about ten. They regarded this as necessary to help them come to grips with their genealogy and past. The parents' reluctance to tell was resented and criticised. They felt very hurt because they could not be trusted with what they felt was their right to know. They regarded their parents' possible fears of losing their children's affections as unjustified, because these were the only people they had feelings for. Truth and honesty, they argued, would have increased their trust and faith in their parents. Most adoptees failed to appreciate the parents' explanation that they were trying to protect them by concealing the truth. They viewed this kind of protection as misguided. The adoptees whose adoption was disclosed to them between the ages of four and eight were the most satisfied. The vast majority thought that the child should be told before the age of ten or eleven and that 'telling' should be geared towards the readiness and needs of each child. Provided that 'telling' was done in a sensitive way any age within the timespan of four to ten seemed to them acceptable. The exact stage of 'telling' did not unduly influence the adoptees' search goals. Other factors have to be examined for an insight into the real reasons for the search.

Though late knowledge of adoption was not clearly associated with the wish to search for the birth parents, 'telling' itself can prove very shattering when it is left till adolescence or adult life. Most adoptees told at this stage went through a period of shock and numbness and later great anger towards their parents for withholding from them. 'Telling' is connected with some deep and complex emotions and because these cannot always be rationally controlled, there will always be some parents who will find it difficult to tell or who may separate 'telling' from feeling. Some of the reluctance to disclose the adoption situation that the study came across had cultural and sub-cultural aspects, as well as being linked with the parents' personal maturity and security.

What was revealed

My mother didn't tell me I was adopted until I was thirteen and had found out accidentally . . . she never, never discussed it again. I tried to ask her once for information about my origins, which I wanted badly, but she did not reply. She made me feel that adoption was something you didn't talk about. I knew I couldn't ask again . . . No, I didn't think of asking my father. Somehow it didn't seem right to ask him; it should be the mother . . . If you don't know the stock you come from you cannot understand yourself. . . .

Female adoptee

The wish to know more about the circumstances of their adoption and about their origins was characteristic of all the adoptees in the sample. This concern about themselves appeared at different stages in their lives, though, for those who already knew, this urge was mostly experienced in adolescence. After the initial shock of revelation, those who came to know about it in adult life desperately wanted to be told more and more as the only possible way they saw of dealing with the upsurge of feeling that the revelation caused. All the adoptees remarked on their need to know about their genealogy in order 'to complete' themselves, aware, as they put it, that they must carry in themselves some aspects from their forebears' characteristics.

According to these adoptees, the fact of being adopted and the wish to explore and understand one's origins is something that appears and reappears all the time depending on new experiences and new relationships. 'Perhaps' one of them remarked, 'this kind of need is with you till death.'

The parental task in adoption appears to be one of helping the child to identify and integrate with two sets of parents. For adoptive parents this is obviously a more complicated task than it is for natural parents. Because of the real existence of two sets of parents the possibility always exists of the adoptee continuing a split between a good and a bad set of parents. Non-adopted children, too, however, have an opportunity of splitting the natural parents into a wholly good and a wholly bad one. Evidence from other areas suggests that under favourable conditions children can be helped gradually to integrate within themselves the idea of two sets of parents. This is similar to the way immigrant children, for instance, under favourable conditions gradually learn to accommodate in their system the idea of two or more cultures with often conflicting values. Many regard the opportunity to integrate positive aspects from more than one culture as enriching. Similarly the few adoptees, in the study, who were introduced to a positive image of their forebears found it a satisfying experience. This did not stop them from occasionally reflecting on their origins but it had not developed into a painful preoccupation. In contrast, adoptees whose parents failed to introduce the idea of another set of parents or who introduced it in a negative form were disturbingly preoccupied with their circumstances and with their genealogy.

The difficulties of most adoptees in the study appeared to result from their failure to build themselves on the notion of two sets of parents with identifiable characteristics. In this they often felt let down by their parents' reluctance to talk about their biological and sociological background. Sometimes they were critical of adoption workers for failing to supply the parents with the relevant information.

The adoptees were asked to say what type of background information they would have liked and also to comment on the desired frequency of discussion.

Type of information desired

The adoptees were generally unanimous that they would have liked information about the circumstances of their adoption, why their original parents gave them up and information about the personal, social and physical characteristics of their natural parents.

By *circumstances of their adoption* they meant such information as: where and exactly when they were born; where and when they were adopted; who made the arrangements and the part played by their natural parents. Of great importance to them was the need to know *why they were given up*, and what circumstances had made it necessary for their parents to surrender them. Especially they would have liked to know whether their parents wanted them or whether they were rejected or abandoned. They saw such information as important to understand themselves or as important to their self-concept.

By *social and personal characteristics* they meant information about their original parents as people; their character and personality, their background, occupation, age at the time of their birth, their interests and hobbies and whether there were any brothers and sisters.

A description of the original parents' *physical characteristics* was felt to be important but not as important as the other aspects of information noted above. They would have been interested to know what their parents looked like, such as: height, colour of hair, eyes, any special physical features or any relevant medical history.

All adoptees saw the sharing of background information as vital and of great importance to themselves and their own children: 'We should not be cut off dead from our origins'; or, 'You want to form a mental picture of your birth-parents like children who had parents who were killed in an accident and who want to know things about them'; or, 'I sit there and say who am I like, I must be like somebody somewhere, who do my children take after?' They associated background information as something that helps 'to complete' one-self but that without it, it is very difficult to do so. 'You feel there is always a gap . . . there is something missing.'

It is difficult to ascertain how much the adoptive parents themselves knew about the personal, social and physical characteristics of the natural parents. There was a period when adoption agencies them-selves were not very keen to pass on such information. As late as 1965 the majority of adoption agencies studied[1] kept little or no record of the characteristics and circumstances of the natural parents. This meant that no, or only very limited, information was passed on to the adopters. If occasionally some information was available about the natural mother there was none about the putative father and nothing about grandparents or great-grandparents. Even if it were made legally possible for adoptees to obtain background information from the agencies that arranged the adoption, the enquiry might end in disappointment because of the paucity of information currently kept.

Though adoptive parents could be ignorant about many aspects of the adoptees' sociological and biological background, there was one area in which they could not feign ignorance. This was the circumstances of and arrangements for the adoption. The general suppression of or reluctance to share other background information extended to this area too.

Frequency of discussion

The adoptees would have generally welcomed not only more frankness but also more discussion about their adoption situation. Frequency is difficult to define, but the adoptees felt that once the child is told without inhibition, background information should be gradually made available to them at a rate that is within the child's capacity to understand and absorb. To shut out the subject following the original revelation only creates the feeling that adoption is 'something to be ashamed of' or 'that it is so awful to be adopted you should not talk about it'.

On the other hand, adoptees would not have liked their parents to stress adoption beyond proportion, or to repeat facts time and again, without sensitivity to and understanding of the adoptees' feelings and readiness to integrate them. Each adoptee appeared to have his or her own pace at which they were ready to absorb and accommodate facts about themselves or about their origins. Some adoptees felt also resentful at the fact that their parents would go round referring to them as their 'adopted son' or 'adopted daughter'. They not only saw it as unnecessary and perhaps hostile but they could see no reason why everyone outside the family should know about their adoption: 'It gave you the feeling of being different from your parents', or, 'It felt like a millstone hanging round your neck.' These adoptees viewed the stressing of 'difference' as a form of rejection.

Puberty and adolescence were the stages at which most of the adoptees experienced an intense desire and curiosity to know more about their origins, 'to understand' themselves, as many put it. Those who only learned about their adoption in adolescence or later were seized with a similar intense desire following the shock of revelation. Even where parents disclosed a certain amount of information before puberty, the adoptees wanted to hear it again and go over it in some detail when they reached adolescence. Whereas discussion during latency seemed to them unimportant, at the adolescent stage they were so preoccupied with themselves, with who they were and with their future, that they were hoping their parents would take the initiative and help them to understand themselves in relation to them and to their birth-parents. Many adoptees said they would have welcomed the opportunity to talk at this stage to someone who knew about the circumstances of their adoption, including an outsider.

Amount of information revealed related to the goals for the current search

From a study of Table 4.1 (see Appendix), a clear pattern emerges which suggests that those adoptees whose adoption was not acknowledged or who were told nothing more besides the fact that they were adopted or who were given some facts but in a hostile way or in a form that depreciated the original parents, were now in significant numbers wanting to *meet their natural parents*. In contrast, adoptees who were given even a fair amount of information in a positive way were predominantly seeking only additional background information.

On the basis of these findings it could be claimed that in general adoptees to whom some information about their original background was revealed, in a sensitive way, were unlikely to be seeking their natural parents. They were more likely to be looking for additional information that they saw as being important in their attempt to understand themselves better. If, however, the adoption was never acknowledged or was enveloped in too much secrecy and evasiveness, or if it was revealed in a hostile way, the likelihood was that the adoptee would be looking for his original parents to provide the answers to his questions and perhaps provide other comforts as well. This observation did not apply to situations where there was a reasonably good relationship but the parents misguidedly withheld information or distorted it, feeling that it was in the child's best interests.

Frequent discussion of the adoption situation was a rather unusual phenomenon. Only about one in every eleven adoptees could claim that there was frequent discussion subsequent to 'telling'. Excepting those cases where hostile remarks were frequently thrown out, in the remaining cases reference to the adoption situation and to the adoptees' background was made once or twice or not at all. The total picture that emerged was one of silence and evasiveness and often of deliberate distortion, sometimes with well-meaning but misguided motives. It is important to stress again that the wish of the adoptees to know more developed mostly during adolescence. Prior to that, there was no or little curiosity.

NATURE OF INFORMATION REVEALED TO ADOPTEES
SEARCHING FOR THEIR NATURAL PARENTS

The great number of adoptees who were now searching for their original parents, either were given no information about their genealogical background, or any information which was given was perceived as hostile to themselves or to their birth-parents. In many instances the parents revealed nothing more besides the fact of adoption. Though the disclosure of adoption gave rise to great curiosity and interest on the part of the adoptees, especially during their adolescence, this need either was not recognised or was rebuffed by the parents. Many of the parents gave the impression that they would not welcome questions or discussion on the subject. A general characteristic of adoptees who were deprived of information about their genealogy and the circumstances of their adoption was an excessive preoccupation with their natural parents and a strong wish to meet them. Mr Erickson, who also found out about his adoption when he went to register at the Labour Exchange, would have liked answers to many questions about his background but at twenty-seven he still could not bring himself to ask his mother:

I don't want to hurt her feelings like, ask her outright what she knows about my natural mother, or if she knows anything about her, or how she came to adopt me; I don't want to go too hard. I said to myself, 'Right enough she would tell me if it was anything terrible', or maybe she is waiting for me to ask. Like I'm waiting for her, giving her the chance to tell me about it, I don't know. This is a puzzle. And yet if I were told earlier and told what she knew about my mother perhaps I wouldn't want to follow on trying to find my other mother . . .

The implication of what most adoptees were saying was that without knowing about one's origins and genealogy it was difficult, if not impossible, to understand oneself or one's abilities, potential or characteristics. One's forebears are an extension of oneself and in the case of the adoptee it extends to two sets of genealogies. A sense of security and belonging was seen by them to be built, among other things, on this kind of extended genealogical identification.

43

The parents of Miss Reid, a professional couple, told her at the age of four but there has been no mention and no discussion around the adoption situation ever since. She was glad that she was told at that age but puzzled by the subsequent avoidance of the subject:

> It felt great at the time but I somehow lost this feeling ever since . . . the secretiveness and the general lack of communication about everything changed all that. . . . Later when I was old enough to understand I was embarrassed to ask for information and perhaps they were embarrassed to tell . . . I expected them and they possibly expected me.

Now at the age of twenty she feels disenchanted with her parents and though they might be able to answer some of her questions she is very reluctant to ask them. She views such a step as creating dependency on her parents which she does not wish.

Another adoptee insisted that every time she tried to ask her parents they brushed it aside:

> But I think they knew an awful lot more than they were willing to say. Nobody talked about it at all, at least not in front of me. Whenever I tried to ask they would clam up and change the subject . . . it makes you feel it is something you ought to be ashamed of, something horrid . . .

Mr Wolfe, who was told when he was fifteen, never discussed his adoption again because he did not get on well with his parents and did not like to hurt or upset them: 'After all they took me into their home and they clothed me and fed me . . . perhaps they didn't know anything more themselves'. Other adoptees did not want 'to intrude' by asking questions whilst some felt that their parents might not be able to take it. One said:

> My parents half told me at the age of twelve after a neighbour's child said I was only an 'adopted bairn'; they made so much fuss then that I felt I could not ask them again . . . I longed to know more and I was hoping they would bring the matter up when I was twenty-one; but they didn't. I do not like it to become an obsession but I feel I must find out now; I cannot postpone it any longer; I feel only half a person without knowing my birth-blood.

Where there was evasion and inhibition adoptees were made to feel that adoption was 'unnatural' or 'something to be ashamed of', or 'something that it isn't nice to talk about'. One adoptee, whose parents were professional people, was not told about his adoption till he was twenty-four. Apart from his 'shattering' experience about the revelation, his parents' attitude left him with the feeling that something was wrong:

> Somehow I felt that they were ashamed to talk about it and
> they gave me the feeling that adoption was unnatural. I felt
> I had to start looking at myself as being different. The subject
> of my adoption was never raised again after that day . . .
> Anyway I was brought up in a very impersonal way and there
> was never much communication between us.

The impression was gained that in some parts of the country adoption is still looked upon as something rather unusual and that those who adopt consider it best either not to tell or to say nothing more besides acknowledging the fact. Miss Grant, now in her early thirties, was told early on that she was adopted but she does not remember any further reference being made to it:

> The fact that I was adopted was slightly hushed which I think
> was a pity. I suppose my mother was brought up in a different
> era when all that kind of thing wasn't quite so normal;
> occasionally it did sound as if she was going to say something
> but one develops a block about these things and perhaps I
> didn't particularly want to hear. I was embarrassed about it I
> suppose and steered her off the track. But looking back it was a
> pity . . . the fact that she didn't encourage me to talk about my
> adoption or tell other people definitely inhibited me—it gave
> me a slight complex about the whole thing and about being
> adopted.

One adoptee who found out about her adoption soon after her wedding, never brought up the subject with her mother:

> I was embarrassed and they were embarrassed. Anything I
> found out I found out from my mother's sister—she doesn't
> know very much but she knows a little. It is too touchy a
> subject to discuss with my mother . . . she would find it
> difficult and at the time I would have found it difficult. Ten
> years have gone by since then and I could talk about it now but
> my mother couldn't. I am quite sure she couldn't. She only

told me once that it was my father's fault; that he was sterile but she had let everyone think that it was her fault she couldn't have any children to save face . . . lots of people do that . . .

Mr Simpson who also discovered about his adoption when he went to register at the Labour Exchange, could not find out more from his mother because she died soon after this:

I have spoken to my father about it once or twice but he just doesn't know anything about it at all. I gathered from him that my mother just wanted another child and she couldn't have one herself, so she adopted me.

A number of adoptees connected their parents' difficulty over talking to them about their adoption with the parents' attitude towards their childlessness, their marital life, to illegitimacy and sex in general. Adoptive parents appeared to shy away from any reference to such topics which possibly had painful implications for them. These adoptees appeared to be sensitive and understanding about their parents' difficulties, whilst at the same time they regretted this inhibition: 'It must have been difficult for them to say that they couldn't have children of their own and to explain why my birth-parents were not married.' Some female adoptees could remember asking their mothers how children were born and were told 'to stop being silly'. When they asked about their adoption they got a similar reply. Others said they wished their parents had shared more about themselves, their families, upbringing, courting and marriage.

A young mother of two children said how she realised early on that her parents had no sexual life of their own:

I thought there was something strange about them. I cannot explain it, but it did not seem natural. My mother did not seem to be a full woman and this must have made a bad effect on their marriage and also made it difficult to talk to me about my adoption and my other parents. Some of my present distress is my mother's lack of interest in me or my children or any children for that matter.

Another young woman made a remark with somewhat similar implications:

When I was pregnant I sensed a great distance between my mother and myself. She showed no enthusiasm and when my little girl was born she remained distant. It was a strange feeling as if it was all too much for her because she had no children herself . . .

Though many adoptees experienced great secrecy and evasiveness from their parents regarding their adoption, it was observed that within most of these families adoption was not the only subject the parents did not talk about. There was no communication or sharing about many other aspects of the parents' past or current life. Some of the adoptees' comments gave indications of the atmosphere at home: 'My mother and father rarely talked about things at home . . . we were not a talking family', or, 'my father was at the pub when he wasn't at work and I saw very little of him'; 'my parents said very few words to each other', or, 'we never talked about personal things'; 'my parents didn't talk about themselves or about their families', or, 'I really know very little about my adoptive parents' past life or how they came to know each other.' The same adoptees who were left ignorant about their origins and genealogy were also left with only a very vague idea about their adoptive parents' life and genealogy. In effect these adoptees were deprived first of information about their real origins and second of distinctive information about their adoptive parents and the latter's forebears. Thus the adoptees' identity was affected by a failure to incorporate within themselves not only the image of the first parents but also of that of the adoptive parents. The lack of communication and the reluctance to tell or to reveal information was not found to be a characteristic of any one social class or of a particular sub-cultural group.

Unlike the majority of adoptees who became very curious, especially in adolescence, a very small number said that once told they did not desire more information until their early twenties. The need for information had been felt recently and it had become a sort of obsession. The main characteristic that distinguished these adoptees from the rest was the very sheltered upbringing they had had. There were indications that they were currently experiencing the curiosity, uncertainties and doubts that are usually associated with adolescence. Belated adolescence is not uncommon in people whose maturing process has for some reason been arrested or delayed.

Where background information was revealed in anger or in ways which depreciated the original parents, and so by implication the adoptees themselves, it raised considerable anxieties and shame.

The adoptees were insistent that only through meeting their original parents would they establish the truth. Insinuations about the natural mother's 'sluttishness', or 'promiscuity' or about 'bastardy' and 'bad blood', or about 'madness' not only were felt as extremely hurting but also raised fears about 'bad blood' and heredity. Adoptees said they would be very distressed to find that their birth-mothers were 'promiscuous' or had abandoned them or that they themselves were the result of a 'one-night stand'. They were prepared to be more understanding if they were to learn that they were the result of a 'steady relationship' or of an 'accident' between two people who loved each other. They would similarly be distressed to hear that they were foundlings or 'nobody's child'.

Some adoptees came to connect their own negative self-image with the bad picture that was constantly painted of their original parents. Most of them being firm believers in heredity, they believed that the 'badness' of their parents might be transmitted to them and through them to their children:

> My mother and I never had much to say to each other. But when she would get cross with me because of something I had done, she would fly into a real temper and she would then say things that really hurt . . . things that I realised then but more now that they were not nice to say to a child . . . she would swear and call me a bastard and say that the way I was shaping I was going to end as a prostitute like my mother. I tried to be careful not to prove her right especially as I couldn't help thinking that it all passes from mother to child . . . Now I am very worried about my daughters who are entering puberty and starting to spread their wings. I hope they will go the right way but if they go the other way I will wonder if there is anything hereditary. I have to face the facts I suppose and try and watch my daughters very carefully, but it is quite agonising.

Similar fears were expressed by other adoptees who, whilst determined to prove their parents' expectations wrong, at the same time were going through real agony feeling that perhaps you cannot get away from heredity and 'bad blood'. The parents of one adoptee would often make reference to promiscuity and the 'bad blood' of illegitimate children. When the adoptee found herself expecting just after she learned about her adoption and had to marry 'hastily', the relatives implied this was 'bad blood' coming out: 'It just crowned it.' The adoptee went on to remark with considerable feeling: 'They will be watching my little girl now to see if she is displaying the same tendencies.'

Another adoptee who only found out about her adoption when already expecting a child out of wedlock, thought that if she had been told earlier about her adoption and her illegitimacy she might not have got into trouble: 'I wouldn't have wanted to have given anyone any room to say, "she must be just like her mother." ' Similar comments were made by others who said they would have avoided certain types of behaviour if they had known in advance that this was a characteristic of their original parents. They wanted to show their adoptive parents and their relatives that they could be different from their first parents.

Two adoptees who happened to have physical marks left on their bodies were wondering if these had been caused by their original parents' cruelty and whether this was why they had been removed from them and 'put up' for adoption. This was something they badly wanted to clarify. One adoptee who has three children of her own cannot stop thinking about the scar on her back and how it came to be there:

> Nobody has told me how the scar on my back came to be there and my adoptive parents are both dead and I cannot ask them . . . Well I couldn't ask them when they were alive because they never wanted to talk about my adoption. But I now have reached the stage when I dread to think about it because my mind turns continuously to my natural mother . . . and if she did this to me is there a danger of me doing the same to one of my children? People say that these things are passed on from parent to child . . .

Being told that the original parent abandoned the child or disappeared or stopped being interested seemed to create strong feelings of rejection and of low self-esteem. This was particularly strong in the few adoptees in the sample who were originally fostered and subsequently adopted by their foster parents. Mrs Thomas was told that her mother had abandoned her to her daily-minder who later adopted her. She felt deeply rejected by her first mother and was pathologically grateful to the adoptive mother for taking her in. She was keen to meet her original mother to establish what she was like as a person and why she had abandoned her. Her concept of herself was largely influenced by what she thought her original mother was like:

> When you first hear of it, it is hard to believe it; I felt very
> bitter and still do. If your own mother did not want you, how
> can you feel good about yourself or not feel bitter? If my mother
> had cared she wouldn't have abandoned me, so I must have
> been unwanted.

Where adoptees learned that a parent kept a previous or subsequent child they felt deeply rejected: 'If she could keep the other child she could have kept me also; obviously she did not want me; this is something very difficult to live with.'

A young adoptee's sole image of his original mother was of 'a mad' woman. Reference to this was usually made when he was being difficult at home. Because of his continued difficulties he was taken into the care of the local authority as being beyond control. The failure of his parents, and perhaps of others, to explain the original mother's illness and to help him clear up his confusion, resulted in considerable fears about himself going mad 'like my birth-mother'. These anxieties and fears generated, among other things, an intense wish to see his mother: 'I must find her and see what she is like; whether she is still ill and what she looks like . . . it is important to see her to be able to understand myself . . .'

This and other adoptees who were presented with only one negative aspect of their parents were left with nothing positive to identify with besides 'madness', 'promiscuity', 'neglectfulness' etc. Apart from the irrelevancy of some of these attributes, there was a failure to project other positive qualities of the original parents.

A number of adoptees in the Meet the Natural Parents group were given some information at the time their adoption was disclosed to them, but the subject was not discussed again and they felt frustrated. A further result of the evasiveness and secrecy that followed was that they gave rise to speculations about the nature of adoption: 'If my parents gave me the opportunity to discuss my adoption with them, it could have helped me to feel that there is nothing wrong with being adopted'; another one remarked, 'It would help my image of myself if my parents had taken me into their confidence more.' These adoptees implied that discussion around the circumstances of their adoption could have afforded a good opportunity to forge closer links between themselves and their parents. Some more perceptive adoptees added, however, that this must be very difficult to do if good ties do not already exist: 'You and your parents must have linked together at some deep level to come to feel that there is enough trust between you to make this kind of sharing possible and uninhibited.'

Adoptees were quick to perceive when their parents felt uneasy, inhibited or embarrassed at having to talk about the adoptive situation. They were very sympathetic towards them but they interpreted this as a message discouraging further discussion. What is of greater interest is that even now in adult life the same adoptees are finding it almost impossible to take the first step and ask for some more information. When the adoptees were young their parents were withholding for fear of hurting them, now that the adoptees were adults they were afraid to broach the subject for fear of hurting their parents.

It was not unusual for some parents to pass on inaccurate bits of information to the adoptee to avoid having to share what they thought were unpalatable facts, such as illegitimacy or the mother's type of occupation. As most of the adoptions studied took place at a period when adoptive applicants were not as numerous as they have been in the last ten to fifteen years, it is very possible that agency workers over-played the child's original background to make it more acceptable to the would-be adopters:

> When I was first told at fifteen, my mother told me a great big story that my natural mother was a teacher and that my father was a business man and because they couldn't marry they gave me up. This was not true. I found out from Register House recently that my mother was only a domestic servant and my father is not even mentioned . . . There was no reason for my parents to lie to me . . .

When the adoptees checked at Register House they were upset to discover that they were given inaccurate facts. They then started questioning the validity and truthfulness of other information given to them. For some it shook their whole confidence in their parents and they were sad and distressed about it: 'If there is one lie there can be a thousand.' Others were more understanding and thought that their parents 'fabricated the information in order to protect me . . . I bear them no grudge'. Mrs Newman, however, was prepared to be more persistent. She was provided with her original name and with her natural mother's name and she was also told that her natural parents were both killed in the last world war. She became suspicious, however, at a later stage when her parents adopted a second child. This child was being told that his original parents were killed in a car crash. She was horrified and distressed because she knew that this was not true and that the child's parents were alive at the time the adoption went through. From this point onward she started doubting her parents' account of the fate of her real parents. There were also other aspects of her family relationships that increased mistrust and unhappiness. For a long time now she has been trying to establish her real origins to find out the truth about herself.

NATURE OF INFORMATION REVEALED TO ADOPTEES
SEARCHING FOR BACKGROUND INFORMATION

The main characteristic that distinguished adoptees searching for background information from those searching for their first parents, was the greater amount of information made available to them about their origins and the circumstances of their adoption. The study showed that the greater the amount of positive genealogical and other similar information made available, the less the involvement and preoccupation with the natural parents. Such adoptees would more likely be looking for information that would help them to complete themselves than be searching for the original parents. Though this group were generally satisfied with the type of information revealed to them they did not consider it adequate and wanted to fill important gaps. They wished strongly that their parents had been more forthcoming and more open, something that they claimed would have made the search unnecessary. Sometimes the parents had no more information in store to give. These adoptees' attitude towards their adoptive parents, compared with the group searching for their natural parents, was generally less critical on this matter and they were more careful to keep their search secret to avoid hurting them. Mrs Hunter, who was adopted into a builder's family, was told about her adoption at the age of about eight or nine. She remembers being told that she was wanted and that her parents could not keep her. When she was about fourteen she felt a sudden need to know more about herself and thought that she could do so only through finding out about her first parents:

> I was a bit apprehensive about asking my mother but I did and she explained to me how I came to them. I was fairly close to

my mother and though she seemed a bit uncomfortable when I asked her, she was quite forthcoming. But she didn't seem to know much about my natural parents or where they came from ... Now that I am expecting my own child I thought it is a good time to find out more through the authorities. But I don't want my parents to know in case they think it reflects on them. I don't want to hurt them as they were good to me and they are the only parents that mean anything to me. But I feel I must find out more about my roots if I am to feel a whole person ...

It could be claimed that when the adoptive parents reveal the adoption situation in a positive way and where they share genealogical information that helps the child to identify with a good image of the natural parents, the likelihood of the adoptee wishing to trace his birth-parents in adult life considerably diminishes.

Mr Wills, who was adopted within his family, had perhaps one of the most constructive experiences from the total sample. The purpose of his current search was to ascertain the exact timing and place of his birth:

So my adopted father spoke to me and explained the circumstances—that he wasn't my natural father and that my natural father, who I always knew as my uncle, used to be my natural father ... I always thought of him as my uncle. My adoptive father gave me the whole story behind it ... My real mother and father, as far as I am concerned, were my adoptive parents ... parenthood is something which is biological but I think at the same time, more than anything else it's psychological. I think the bond is deep but it's deep in a personal relationship rather than a biological ... I remember my father referring to it from time to time throughout the years. [The adoptive mother died soon after the revelation of adoption.] My adoptive father could speak of my original mother and father, but especially of my mother who was dead, and he would speak of her with affection. Although I had never known my real mother, somehow or other I got to know her through my father. No, I don't think the age of ten is late to tell. This was a good time for me, it may not suit everybody ...

Another adoptee who was now seeking more particulars said that possibly his parents told him everything they knew, but he was curious to see whether Register House could provide him with any more detailed information:

> My parents were very honest and they never gave me the impression of trying to conceal anything from me. They told me when I was eight or nine and this age suited me. They also made it clear that I had another mother and father and that they adopted me because they could not have children and that my real parents could not keep me. They said something about me being kept by my grandmother and that the adoption was arranged through a solicitor . . . If I wanted to talk about my adoption there was no evasion but I do not think they could really fill in important details because they did not know.

Though Mrs Young found out about her adoption when she was twenty and was told very little about it she did not seem to see it as unusual.

> I would have liked to know something about my original parents but the subject was not touched at home. No, it doesn't surprise me . . . you see we are not a talking family . . . we don't talk about personal things like this. My parents should have told me about my adoption earlier but I don't see what else they could do. It must be difficult to know what to tell an adopted person. There have been times when I wondered and felt curious about my birth-people but it did not really bother me until recently.

A very small number of other adoptees in this group who were given very little information about their origins were not unusually critical of their parents' withholding. They were convinced that their parents were trying to protect them by not raising this painful subject and they could not blame them for that. But a number of events had recently made them feel curious about their forebears and a strong desire 'to tie loose ends'.

Summary

Most of the adoptees in the sample were given very little or no information about their original background. There was also very little or no discussion of their adoptive situation subsequent to its disclosure. Ideally all adoptees would have liked to know about the circumstances of their adoption, why they were surrendered, and to have information about the personal, social and physical characteristics of their natural parents. Each adoptee placed different emphasis on some items of information than others but the over-all picture was an intense interest in their genealogy. They would have liked their parents to tell them early, simply and with honesty and to tell them a fair amount about their background. They did not necessarily expect them to tell the whole story at one go but to gear information and its timing to the developing interests and needs of each child. Real curiosity was mostly awakened around adolescence. Before that there seemed to be a lack of interest in their genealogy. Most of them, whilst being critical of the evasiveness and secrecy adopted by their parents, were also understanding about the possible insecurity the latter may have been going through. They generally wished that their parents had trusted them more and taken them more into their confidence. The lack of trust and honesty was viewed by adoptees as unfortunate and distressing.

In general adoptees who were given no information about their origins and those who were given some information but in a way which depreciated the original parents were predominantly wanting to meet their natural parents. In contrast, those who were given some information in a positive and understanding way were mostly interested in additional particulars about their origins.

5   Perception of family relationships

I had a peculiar life. I cannot tell you exactly. My mother and my father I liked a lot but it is unfortunate that my mother didn't know how to give and my father was the same. I didn't want material things in life but love. Every child needs a mother's love that makes them secure in life but I didn't have it. My mother and I were never close together. She found it hard to show affection to people. She was not a soft person. Maybe she is different underneath but this I don't know. There was no real family life in our house . . . I really shouldn't run them down because they have been good to me but although I was brought up by them I was not really part of them . . .

Young female adoptee

Adoptees were generally keen to talk about their lives as adopted people and especially about the quality of their relationships within their adoptive homes. It is realised that the adoptees' own account of the quality of their home life is a very subjective experience and therefore not necessarily always accurate. What was real was many adoptees' distress, sadness or emotional stress and the fact that they tended to attribute these feelings either to their being adopted or to the kind of upbringing they had had or, more frequently, to both. It is recognised that misperceptions and distortions of experiences are common phenomena where human relationships are involved. It is also possible that under the impact of new stresses arising out of current life situations, the quality of earlier relationships may have been clouded or distorted. Because people in general, not necessarily adopted ones, have mixed feelings about even the best relationships, it may be that the negative aspects appear to predominate only under the impact of very stressful events. Anxieties and bad feelings triggered by such crises may then be projected onto people of emotional significance to the individual. This, for example, appeared to have happened in certain cases of bereavement and of delayed adolescent reactions. However, the consistency and repetitiveness of certain comments made by different adoptees, especially about adverse experiences within their adoptive families, cannot be explained entirely by misperceptions and distortions.

With few exceptions, even adoptees who were feeling critical of their parents could also display positive feelings towards them, and a fair amount of loyalty and respect. Where it was implied that there was an absence of an emotional bond between the adoptees and their parents, the former still felt obligated to their parents for 'taking them in', for 'not being left in an institution', or for 'being sent to a good school'. They continued to view their adoptive parents as their sole parents and only a very small number of very unhappy persons felt so strongly that they wanted to sever all connections with them.

When adoptees felt critical of their home life, their negative feelings usually went well beyond what one expects to find in any reasonable relationship. Angry feelings were often strong and usually accompanied by bitterness and disillusionment. Some of the adoptees who felt in this way believed that life with their natural parents or even a different set of adoptive parents might have been infinitely better.

The over-all impression was that the adoptees badly wanted to identify with their adoptive parents and be like them. Where they were not entirely successful there was more sadness than bitterness, except in extreme cases of perceived neglect. Even in the most successful cases of positive identification, however, it rarely extended to the parents' genealogy beyond those in the immediate family circle. In other words the adoptees implied a difficulty to conceptualise and align themselves with the adoptive parents' genealogical background.

Adoptees who saw their adoptions as a total failure tended to attribute all the bad bits in themselves to their adoptive parents and all the good parts to their original ones. Warmth, spontaneity, kindness, intelligence, verbal expression and various skills were seen to have been inherited from the original parents whilst 'unhappiness', 'emptiness', lack of achievement, inability to love and so on were viewed as being the direct result of adverse conditions within their adoptive homes. Some adoptees were critical of their parents' unreasonable expectations of them, whilst others complained of not being 'pressed' hard enough.

The adoptees' description of their home life and their views about its quality, closely coincided with their perception of their own personal adjustment and well-being (see chapter 6). Broadly, adoptees who saw themselves as unhappy and unsettled said that their adoptive lives were unsatisfactory; these adoptees were almost exclusively searching for their original parents (see Appendix: Table 5.1). Those adoptees who described themselves as fairly 'contented' individuals with no obvious difficulties in coping with life situations, their jobs, or children, generally perceived their adoptions as having been more satisfactory; adoptees in this latter group were predominantly searching for additional background information (Table 5.1). In between these two extreme groups there was the group of adoptees who perceived both themselves and their adoptions as having been 'fairly happy' or 'fairly successful'; these adoptees could be searching either for their original parents or for more background information.

Almost half the adoptees perceived their adoptive home relationships as having been unsatisfactory and their adoption as a failure or mainly a failure. Over half of these had received psychiatric help at some stage in their lives, whilst only an insignificant number of those who perceived their adoptions as a success had done so. Another 28 per cent perceived their adoption and family relationships as fairly satisfactory whilst the rest (26 per cent) described it as mainly satisfactory (Table 5.1). Even some of those who described their adoption as satisfactory were critical of certain aspects of it, such as their parents' evasiveness, or secretiveness. Social class differences or differences in the age of adoptive parents at placement did not appear to be related to the adoptees' perception of the quality of their home life. Adoptees, however, whose parents were fifty or over at the time of placement, expressed dissatisfaction about the age differential.

Significantly more adoptees expressed dissatisfaction with their mothers than their fathers. In the same way that it was the mother they mainly expected to do the 'telling' and give information, they also generally expected the mother to be the one responsible for maintaining a happy home life. A possible explanation for this is that mothers rather than fathers are associated with warmth, love and comfort and where these qualities are lacking the mother is the one to be criticised. A further explanation is that the adoptive mother is perhaps identified with the natural one. She becomes the receptacle not only for negative feelings because of her failure to provide 'good enough' mothering but also for negative feelings that belong to the natural mother. In some extreme cases the adoptees split the two mothers by seeing the adoptive one as the totally 'bad' whilst idealising the natural mother.

Whether the adoptee was an only child or a member of a family with younger or older siblings, adopted or non-adopted ones, appeared to have no bearing on his perception of the quality of his home life. A most reassuring observation was the general closeness between siblings, adopted or otherwise. Only one adoptee, who was adopted in a family with own children who were considerably older than himself, said that his siblings would sometimes say 'my mother' or 'my father' and not 'our mother or father'; yet he himself was referred to by them as the 'favourite'.

Before these findings are seen out of context, it should be stressed again that the analysis presented here refers to the relationships of those adoptees who felt the need to delve into their genealogical background and not to that of adopted people and their parents in general.

The adoptees' perception of their family relationship related to the aims of their search

Almost all adoptees who described their home life and family relationships as unsatisfactory were now searching for their original parents, whilst a significant number of those who perceived their family relationships as satisfactory was searching mainly for background information (Table 5.1). Similarly a significant majority of the adoptees who said that their home life was 'fairly' or 'reasonably' satisfactory was searching for background information, whilst the rest were looking for their original parents. In the three cases where the adoptive relationship was perceived as unsatisfactory but the adoptees were only searching for background information, in the first, there was evidence that the natural parents had deserted, and the adoptee felt so rejected that she said she could not bring herself to meet them. In the second, there was concrete information that the natural mother was dead and, in the third, the adoptee was very cross with her natural mother for not making sure that she had been placed in a good home. Because of her strong feelings towards her birth-mother she did not wish to trace her as she did not believe she would have anything to offer her.

The six adoptees who, though the relationship with their parents was described as satisfactory, were now trying to meet their first pair of parents were people who had recently been faced with some acute crisis. Moreover, because one or both of the adoptive parents was dead, their first impulse was to seek the original ones for comfort. With the crisis over, their motivation also subsided.

Overall, the findings pointed to the importance and quality of family relationships as the primal force that determined the search and influenced its objectives. A gradation scale built on the basis of these findings showed that with the worsening of the quality of the family relationships there was an increase in the desire to meet the natural parents. The attitude of the parents to such issues as timing of revelation, frequency of discussion and information shared was mostly but not always influenced by the quality of relationships prevailing in the home.

The quality of the adoptees' home life and the timing of the adoption revelation

Adoptees who were told before the age of eleven expressed greater satisfaction with their home life than those who were told or found out later. Early 'telling', however, was not always an indication of satisfying relationships prevailing within the home any more than late revelation was always the sign of insecure and impoverished relationships.

Early 'telling' was seen by some parents as a duty to be performed and by others it was done in a hostile and vindictive form. The reluctance of some others to tell was connected with local tradition which supported 'not telling' as being in the best interests of the child. A few parents came to genuinely believe that it would be damaging to the child to know either the fact of his adoption or the real circumstances of his parents. Once it had been left very late and usually after the adoptee had been informed by outside sources, the parents as well as the child found themselves unable to discuss the matter beyond an acknowledgment of the facts. Sometimes, by the time the adoptee knew, one or both parents were dead and not available to answer the questions.

The quality of the adoptees' home life related to the amount of background information revealed

The amount of background information revealed by the parents was mainly a reflection of the quality of the relationships as perceived

by the adoptees. The findings showed that the adoptees who perceived their home life as unsatisfactory had generally been given no
information about their origins or only hostile and depreciative
facts about the natural parents (see Appendix: Table 5.2). There
were some exceptions to this finding in that some adoptees who were
given no information at all, still perceived their adoptive relationships as fair to satisfactory. Like 'telling', where some well-meaning
parents held back, these same parents also withheld information,
either because they thought it would be damaging to the child or they
had nothing to reveal. Satisfactory relationships were predominantly
accompanied by the revelation of a fair amount of information,
though even within some such relationships, no background information was made available, and in a very small number the adoption
itself was not acknowledged.

*The adoptees' perception of their home life related to the timing of the
placement*

The adoptees who were placed with their families when a year old or
more, mostly perceived their home life as unsatisfactory and their
adoptions as a failure. Of sixteen such adoptees, thirteen described
their adoptive home life as totally unsatisfactory, two as partly
satisfactory and only one said that he had a happy home life. Of the
sixteen who were placed when a year old or more, fourteen were now
searching for their original parents and only two for background
information. No association was found between earlier placement
and the adoptees' perception of their home life or search goals.

The association between late placement and unsatisfactory relationships suggests that in any discussion about the factors contributing
to failure in adoptive family relationships, the child's experiences
before placement would need to be considered.

HOW ADOPTEES SEARCHING FOR THEIR BIRTH PARENTS PERCEIVED
THEIR HOME LIFE

It was stated earlier that almost all adoptees who perceived their
adoptions as unsatisfactory and just over half of those who perceived
them as partly satisfactory were aiming to meet their original parents.
Unsatisfactory home situations were generally described as 'lacking
in love', 'devoid of warmth and real caring', 'impersonal', containing

'very controlled people who could not display feelings', 'disturbed or neurotic people adopting for their own needs' so that adoptees 'never felt close to them', and experienced 'rows, quarrels and arguing' and 'verbal abuse about my background'. There were only two cases of actual physical neglect whilst in most of the rest the criticism was one of emotional neglect, lack of communication and of sterile relationships. A typical experience was that of Miss Bell, a girl in her late teens. Miss Bell was now looking for her original mother, hoping she would find a shoulder on which to lay her head. Though her adoptive parents always provided her with everything she needed, she maintained that neither could show or invite any emotion:

> I was always envious of other children whose mothers would hug and kiss them and play with them. My mother seemed always unresponsive and distant. I lost my father when I was eleven. My mother committed suicide the day after she told me I was adopted. I was then only twelve and I felt terrible and entirely lost. I was desperate and unhappy with no one to turn to. My loneliness and misery have been increasing ever since. Perhaps my mother could not give more or respond . . . she must have been a very unhappy person like I am now. Following her death some of the relatives rallied round and tried to be nice but after the first few weeks we couldn't get on together. They were very strict and could not understand my feelings . . . they expected me to feel happy and pleased though I was miserable. There was no real feeling for me. They were not cruel but just could not accept me for what I was. Because of our arguments I went into a Children's Home when I was twelve. I felt that nobody wanted me . . . I still have no one to turn to.

It was characteristic of adoptees who felt unloved or distant from their parents and who did not feel they belonged, to transfer similar feelings towards other people in their immediate environment, including relatives. A number of other adoptees in this group felt they could never be loved enough because of their 'emotional hunger'. Subsequent relationships seemed to confirm this feeling because of their lack of satisfaction. Mr Craig was placed with his parents when he was only six weeks old but he was now feeling disillusioned and disappointed with his family and with himself. He blamed his adoption and his experiences for his present feelings and outlook. The loss of his father when he was only six left him with a sense of irreparable loss and with a vacuum in his life. He was very critical of the 'welfare' for placing him in a home where the father was suffering from a deteriorating condition and where the mother, he maintained, was neurotic and unstable. He attributed his general sense of insecurity and 'nerves' to his mother's inability 'to love' him and to make him feel 'wanted':

> She was a very rejecting and unloving woman; when angry she would call me names about my background and my adoption and say that she regretted having me. I now think that she was unwell mentally and not suitable to have any children adopted or not adopted . . . I was not an easy child but she never gave me and my brother and sister any affection. I have been going through life hoping to find this and obviously my natural mother was my main hope.

He went on to express equally bitter feelings about his first mother for giving him up without ensuring first that he was going into a 'good' home. Though he was earnestly looking for her, he was also feeling rather hostile and unforgiving towards her.

Mrs Jenkins, now a married woman in her late twenties, was placed at the age of three months. She talked of her 'neglect' by parents who, she thinks, stayed together only because of her:

> I never felt cherished or made to feel good in myself. I never really fitted into my family. They were agricultural workers and we lived in a small community. They seemed to work hard but my memories are of my father and sometimes my mother coming home drunk. On Saturdays my parents would go out drinking and they would either leave me at home or drop me at the cinema. There was always a fight on Saturday evenings and somebody got smacked. My schooling was also very sadly neglected. Monday mornings depended on whether there was enough money left from Saturday night to give me lunch money. People never took sandwiches in that part of the country—so I would stay away from school. My parents were taken to court several times for not sending me to school. Because of my father's drinking and my mother's attitude, I never brought a friend home; I was ashamed. People often ask me, 'How are your mum and dad?' and I say, 'I don't have a mum and dad, I'm adopted.'

When interviewed, Mrs Stone was feeling 'miserable and unhappy' and had asked her family doctor for help. Though a married woman with children, she was still very preoccupied and involved with her origins and her adoption. She was critical of the adoption agency which placed her with a couple that turned out not to be married though the adoption order was made in the name of both 'parents'. The 'father' deserted soon after the adoption was completed and he never returned. She talked of her unhappy upbringing by an 'unloving' mother and about the frequent fights and quarrels they had. The first time she knew of her adoption was when her mother threatened to send her back to her original mother. The adoptee maintained that there was frequent reference to her 'slut mother' and how she herself would one day follow in her mother's steps. When she reached sixteen she left home and shortly afterwards became pregnant:

> Everybody then kept talking about my 'bad blood' and I was convinced that it was my mother's 'bad blood' showing. My adoptive mother didn't want me at home. I was hoping she would soften and show some kindness but she never did. I had to go into a Mother and Baby Home and in spite of what happened to me, eventually I put my own child up for adoption. I couldn't have done otherwise . . .

The estrangement of another female adoptee from her family was expressed through her determination to change her surname to leave 'no trace' of her adoption and to 'obliterate' her connection with her adoptive family. She was placed with them at the age of three but now she wanted to believe that she had no 'Scottish blood', like her adoptive family, and that she was very different from them. She attributed her current confusion and general depression to what she thought was a 'sterile upbringing'.

> They were not what real parents should be; I was never close to them and I received no encouragement to get close to them. They were very controlled people and lacked warmth. They were not harsh or anything of that sort, only empty of feelings. They couldn't make you feel wanted and needed . . . I suppose I am a bit like them now. When my father died I could not shed a tear. I had no feelings for him and I have none for my mother either. I would not shed a tear if she died tomorrow . . .

Other adoptees who were mostly critical of their parents described
how the death of a parent had not touched them or had left them
unmoved. Though some regretted the fact that they could not feel
anything, they remarked how they could not have behaved differently
because of what they were. A male adoptee remarked:

> Myself I never felt close to anybody. When my granny died I
> did not feel anything. I felt little when my father died and when
> my mother died recently I did not feel a thing. I never felt close
> to anyone to love, or to confide, either father or mother . . .
> mine was an unhappy adoption. I felt as an outsider and my
> relatives saw me as an outsider too.

Dissatisfaction and disillusionment left some adoptees wondering
whether it might not have been preferable to have grown up in an
institution:

> I never understood what family life was like and there was no
> love or care. My adoptive father never really wanted me and it
> was only to please my mother. They took me in from the
> Corporation as a foster child first. It used to hurt very much
> when my father would often address me with sarcasm as 'Sir' . . .
> They seemed kinder to the girl they fostered. My mother is now
> old and sick but I cannot bring myself to visit her. I have no
> feelings for them . . . it may be cruel but this is how I feel. I
> would never like anyone to go through what I went with my
> life and adoption . . . I used to envy other children at school
> for the way their parents looked after them. My adoption though
> taught me one thing: that it is up to you to make your way in
> life. You must depend only on yourself.

Mrs Newman was two years old when she was placed with her
parents. Prior to that she had two foster homes. She too described
what appeared to be very unhappy and sometimes cruel experiences
but she was less bitter and was prepared to be understanding:

> I wouldn't say I had a happy adoption all the way through
> really; I can remember back about as far as when I was four
> years old . . . my parents expected a very high standard of me
> because of my father being a very intelligent man . . . Of course
> when I didn't do my work properly he used to hit me . . . he
> used to hit me with a swagger cane; he used to hit me on the
> knuckles and he used to hit me in other places with it . . . My

mother, too, would lose her temper with me because I was not very bright. One day something went wrong with some maths or something and she had a pair of scissors and she picked them up and she threw them at me. She caught me just here and in fact I've still got the mark where the scissors went in. My parents never seemed to get on all that well together, there was always rows, rows and rows . . . when I look on it now it was perhaps not me they were getting at, it was friction among themselves and taking it out on me . . . Yet when I think of parents the only two people I think of is my parents who brought me up . . . your mother is your mother who brought you up whether its your real mother or not . . .

The single-parent family

Being brought up by a single parent, either because the latter was not married or because of widowhood or separation, was generally perceived as unsatisfactory. Six of the nine adoptees who were brought up under such conditions were critical of the arrangements and described their adoptions as 'unnatural' or 'incomplete'. The remaining three were less critical because of the way they were looked after and cared for by the single parent. They found it helpful being members of an extended family which included uncles, cousins and grandparents who, according to these adoptees, made up for the absence of a father. They maintained, however, that if they had a choice they would prefer a family with a father and mother.

Mrs Driver, a young mother with a psychiatric history, had been placed with a widow at the age of one year. Her mother did not reveal her adoption to her and when she found out at the age of fourteen she avoided telling her mother:

I always felt there was something lacking in this family of two women. There were no relatives or anyone we knew around. My mother's own defective son was in an institution and I suppose I was adopted to make up for the loneliness. Somehow it didn't feel right to me. There was no affection or care. We had to live frugally on the pension. I never felt loved and I am aware that I cannot love my own children now. If your adoption is unhappy it makes it more difficult to feel of your adoptive parents as a family. I could not muster any feelings for my mother when she died two years ago. It is an awful thing to say but I feel I have no parents, the word 'mother' shocks me every time I say it . . .

In spite of Mrs Driver's unhappiness and disappointment, when her mother died she felt 'more desolate, unloved and unwanted'. The death of her mother was seen by her as a further loss and abandonment reinforcing perhaps similar feelings about her original mother whom she was now desperately seeking.

A young professional woman who was adopted by her widowed grandmother was brought up knowing of her adoptive status. The grandmother was described as kind but the adoptee still regretted the arrangement:

I envied other children who had both parents. I grew up having never called anyone father or mother but only grandma . . . when my own child now calls me mother the word sounds unreal and stirs no immediate reaction; I know because my husband seems to react differently.

Another adoptee, who was brought up by a single woman and her brother, found it very difficult to reconcile herself to calling them 'mother' and 'father' after she understood that they could not have been her parents because they were only brother and sister and not husband and wife:

This was all wrong. I mean I really had a terrible life because I couldn't understand it. Other children would say: 'How can they be your mother and father without being married?' It made me feel that mine was not a family like other people's and that there was no proper family to have me. I was miserable and emotionally upset all the time . . .

In spite of these feelings and of her bitterness towards 'the welfare' for making the arrangements, this adoptee only started searching for her original parents when both her adoptive ones died: 'I would have had it on my conscience otherwise; after all they did keep me even if they did not give me anything much more. It would have been all wrong to try and hurt them.'

The blood-tie

Adoptees who were very critical of their adoptive families were generally firm believers in the blood-tie bond and they were convinced that 'blood is thicker than water' or 'there is nothing like your own flesh and blood'. This argument was mostly used to demonstrate

67

their alienation from their adoptive families. Children who are not adopted, and come to feel likewise, must find other areas on which to focus their discontent. But in adoption it could in reality have been different. One young student who fell out with her parents and was very critical of their 'unemotional response' remarked:

> I think that adopted children are like their real parents. I do not care what everybody else says . . . your character is formed through your heredity . . . I don't think adopted children grow up according to the background of their adopted family . . . I wouldn't like to think that I have taken after the character of my adoptive family . . .

Another adoptee who was similarly convinced that the blood-tie is the only bond that matters, changed his views drastically after meeting his original mother. Now he is certain that it is the people who bring you up that matter. A woman who recently had her first baby couldn't believe that anyone can be as meaningful to a child as the people who bear and give birth to it.

In contrast, adoptees who felt that their adoption was a reasonably successful one, attached greater importance to the beneficial effects of environmental factors and were glad about identifiable traits in themselves which they had acquired from their adoptive parents.

Other adoptees, in their efforts to find areas on which to focus their criticisms, disapproved of the fact that their adoptive parents were above their original ones in socio-economic status, but others felt the opposite. Whilst some were bitter about their parents being 'ignorant working-class people' or 'lacking in culture', others were equally critical of having been placed with 'upper-class snobs' or with people interested only in what the neighbours would say. One said: 'Why should I, from a mining background, be placed with these rich merchants?' There was no evidence from the study that socio-economic differences as such were responsible for the adoptees' feeling of distance between themselves and their adoptive parents. As it was only recently that they had become aware of the different socio-economic backgrounds of their adoptive and original parents, the importance of such factors can be discounted, except in as far as they were an obvious area to focus negative feelings on.

A number of adoptees, who perceived their adoptions as only partly successful, could at the same time see certain positive aspects in them that had made them tolerable. They were generally less bitter and disillusioned than those who said that their home life had been unsatisfactory. One male adoptee who attributed his own general 'unhappiness' and 'nerves' to the emotional neglect of his parents went on to add:

> My mum and dad were committee people; they never stayed at home much and did not show much interest in myself or my sister. Ours was a kind of impersonal upbringing. I longed as a child to see more of them but they were not family people . . . they were not cruel or anything like that they simply never had time. I suppose they thought that the nanny we had was sufficient for us. Yet when I reflect upon it it was better perhaps than being brought up in an orphanage. I would say my adoption was fairly happy. What would I be if I were not adopted?

Mrs Drummond saw her adoption as neither 'disastrous nor happy'. She never felt she belonged and found her mother 'cold' and difficult to talk to. She could talk more easily to her father and when he died she was very upset. She saw her 'intelligence' and 'warmth' as coming from her natural parents.

> What was lacking was a bond. There was just no love and no feeling. I mean my mother was just a person. I would now do anything to help her but mainly out of duty. She did bring me up after all. I was sent to a good school and what have you, but I just don't know—it's peculiar, I can't put my feelings into words . . . I wish I could feel more for her.

Mrs Donald was adopted as a child by a professional couple whose marriage broke up when she was about two. Money was tight, depending on the father's remittances, but Mrs Donald's real regret was her incomplete family life:

> In a way I think that my natural mother obviously thought she was having me adopted because I would have a nice stable home, something she could not give me . . . but it was anything but a stable home. My natural mother would have probably had a fit if she'd known the circumstances . . . My own fear as a child was that if anything happened to my adoptive mother, because we had nobody else, we would just have been out on a limb. I certainly missed not having my father at home because I was very fond of him but he opted out of the upbringing of us. My

mother tried to be good to us, myself and my brother—her own son—but she was too over-protective and too anxious for us . . .

One of the major characteristics of many adoptees in this group was the way in which they often split the adoptive parents into wholly good or wholly bad ones. Frequently it was the mother who was seen as the wholly bad figure whilst the father was kept as a 'good' figure. In most of the cases where one of the parents had died, strong negative feelings were projected onto the surviving one. Where the surviving parent happened to re-marry, either when the adoptee was young or even later in life, this was seen as 'abandonment' or 'rejection' and was accompanied by real anger and hostility towards the parent. One possible explanation is that the loss of a parent reactivates feelings about the original loss and 'abandonment' by the natural parent(s) but because the natural parent, as well as the dead adoptive one, is somewhat idealised, all the negative feelings are projected onto the surviving one. Where the latter re-marries, the 'abandonment' is experienced as complete. On the death of a parent, not only does the adoptee re-experience a strong sense of loss but he or she expects considerable comfort and support from the surviving parent. If, however, the latter is preoccupied with his or her own mourning process or because of personality factors fails to give the expected response, then bitterness and disillusionment follow.

Mrs Sharp lost her father when she was sixteen. Since then she has been at odds with her mother whom she criticises for being 'unloving' and 'uncaring' and not interested in her and her children. She was attached to her father whom she saw as 'pleasant and quiet', whilst she saw her mother as 'rigid' and 'outdated'. Since her father's death she cannot tolerate her mother even touching her. Unlike her feelings for her father, she never felt close to her mother; they 'never struck it together'. She blames her mother for her feeling 'empty and isolated' in herself. Her husband's query, why she does not value his love and support, elicited the response that 'no one can make up for a parent's love'.

HOW ADOPTEES IN SEARCH OF BACKGROUND INFORMATION PERCEIVED THEIR FAMILY RELATIONSHIPS

In contrast to adoptees who perceived their adoptions as predominantly unsatisfactory and who were now searching for their first parents, those who saw their family relationships and adoptive outcome as mainly satisfactory were mostly searching for background information. They were still somewhat critical of their parents for not being more open and honest about the facts surrounding their adoption, but the relationship between themselves and their parents seemed strong enough to survive such disappointments and criticisms. Good relationships were described as 'loving', with the adoptee 'made to feel that I belonged', with 'plenty of relatives around', 'abundance of love', 'kindness'; or, 'my adoption was made successful because of the love of my parents.' These adoptees regarded their current search as an attempt to fill in gaps about their genealogy, or to complete themselves or 'to tie loose ends'. Even where the adoptees' home life seemed a fairly happy one, there was still the desire to know as much as possible about their forebears and the sociological history of their family.

A young professional man, who was brought up as an only child, was told about his adoption at the age of ten and thought it was the best time for him. He talked with great respect about his parents whom he described as 'caring and affectionate'. He had a happy home life with both his parents being actively involved in his upbringing:

> I was made to feel that I belonged and I never thought of them
> as adoptive parents but as parents. I never felt the lack of a
> blood-tie and I think of myself as having had a good home life.
> My parents' relatives are my relatives and when I think of
> parents and family I don't think of my birth-parents. But
> learning more about my forebears should help me to complete
> myself.

The father of this young man died when the latter was fifteen. He coped with the loss by identifying with a lot of his father's interests and hobbies. Unlike some other adoptees, who at the death of one parent split their conception of both into one wholly good and one wholly bad, he seemed to maintain a reasonable relationship with his mother whilst cherishing good memories of his father. The parents gave him a fair amount of information about his background, but he was hoping to find out more from the search. He was concerned that his mother should not know about his search for fear of upsetting her.

Unlike the group of adoptees who were critical of their adoptions, this group felt part of their parents' family—aunts, uncles, cousins, etc. They found their relations like 'everyone else's' and did not think of them as not being real relatives. One of them remarked how being adopted never posed any problem to her:

It never stood in my way—my parents and my brother made my adoption a very happy one. We had plenty of relatives and our relationships were and still are wonderful . . . if you learn to get on with people they don't have to be of your own flesh . . . it is how you feel that matters and not who you are.

Miss Black was very glad to have been brought up in a family with many nieces and nephews living near by: 'I've got a large family by adoption which is nice. I look upon them as my family.' Like some other adoptees who were brought up as only children, she wished she had siblings so that she would feel less exposed. She reiterated the views of other adoptees who were brought up as single children by saying: 'In adoption you start with a limited family and it is very easy, once your parents are dead, to feel a bit out on a limb. Parents should be encouraged to adopt more than one child'.

Mr Muir was adopted when a child by a family who had an older child of their own. He found out about his adoption when he was nine and though his parents acknowledged it nothing more was said. In spite of his regrets about their silence he still speaks with enthusiasm about his adoption:

I had a very happy adoption because of a very good relationship with my mother. She had a tremendous amount of love and affection for me. There was an abundance of love and care for me and my sister. My father became blind early on and he had to rely on me a lot . . . Him I respected very much because he was a kind man. Everybody made me feel I belonged. When I visit my relatives or when they visit me, I don't think of them as non-blood relations . . . But I now feel that there are things I don't know about my origins and I would like to find out. No disrespect is meant to my parents. If I don't find out what I am looking for, I will leave it at that . . .

In spite of the drawbacks noted earlier about adoptions by single people, Miss Grant, a young teacher, had many positive feelings towards her mother, though as a whole she was not in favour of adoptions by single parents. She attributed her own satisfaction to the kind of person her 'mother' was and to the big family of relations that surrounded her:

> She was a wonderful person and I think it was her character and personality that persuaded the authorities that she was a suitable person . . . She was more like a grandparent but she did pretty well. I was very happy. Obviously one misses out on certain things but then if you think of the number of people who perhaps lose their fathers when they are quite young, the situation isn't really all that much different. One misses out on the family life but I was lucky in having lots of cousins who brought me up more like brothers and sisters . . . we were a happy and closely knit family. But I never called her 'mother' because she was a spinster and it would have been awkward if I did. If you are adopted by a couple, as most people are, you can say my father does this or that. Not having a mother and father to lay hands on immediately you have got to tell people right away that you are adopted and I found that a bit difficult . . . But what I really missed out on is not seeing a happy relationship between parents as man and woman . . .

As an indication of the sense of belonging that a good relationship can create, it is appropriate to quote from the remarks of one adoptee whose current search was of a more practical nature. He is in his late twenties and he was told about his adoption when he was ten:

> To me my adoptive parents are my mum and dad and I love them dearly. We had a very good relationship which was built over a long period—it was a real thing and not artificial. I think it is wrong for anyone to suggest that adoptive relationships can never be as real as natural ones. Well, some people think there is nothing like a blood-tie: I think, from my own experience, that it's a lot of nonsense. My adoption was made successful because of the love of my parents. If a child knows that it is loved, that is all that matters. That is the most important bond. All the way through I had a sense of belonging to them. I think a personal relationship is more important than the biological one, I really do. Let's face it, a biological relationship is sometimes purely accidental—it's a matter of what happened one night, so to speak. But a personal relationship is something which is built up over the years and because of this it is a lasting one.

73

Perception of family relationships

When his mother died whilst in his teens he felt it as a tremendous loss but this loss was not experienced as 'rejection' or 'abandonment' as was implied by other adoptees who went through similar situations but whose family relationships were less satisfactory. He added:

> To me it was the loss of a real mother—it was a terrible blow which took me a long time to get over, but I think this was the measure of our relationship . . . it helped me being also close to my father. I drew a lot of comfort from him. When he died four years ago I realised how much I missed him. Both my parents meant a great deal to me.

Relationship difficulties

Unhappiness resulting from poor home life and from emotional neglect is not of course peculiar to certain adoption situations. Practitioners in the caring professions frequently come across non-adopted people who feel equally distressed and who have experienced equally sterile relationships. Many of the adoptees who were disillusioned with their home life also described themselves as mostly unhappy or as being under considerable stress which they attributed to their family relationships or to the fact of being adopted. It is difficult to disentangle the etiological factors for the disturbed relationships experienced by these adoptees; how far these were, for instance, the result of personality difficulties in the parents, or of constitutional and personality factors in the child which adversely influenced the developmental processes. In discussing the etiology of psychological difficulties in adopted children Dr Gerard[1] writes:

> Deviations are due to a variety of causes, which may operate at any or all stages of development . . . development occurs as 'the interaction between the maturational processes and environmental influences'. In the discussion of the development and treatment of any abnormal condition, one must consider the role which each element plays in its creation. Both the conditions of maturation and the environmental situations are changing from time to time. Yet there are certain relative constants which form the framework around which these changes occur. . . One of these constants is the constitutional

inheritance of the child . . . Of less constancy than the constitution of an individual are the personalities of the child's mother, father and other people in the environment . . .

Besides the constitutional and family environmental factors which represent continuing influences on personality development, other accidental and less predictable influences also play important roles. Traumatic experiences, considered at first by Breuer and Freud as the essential causes of the neuroses, no longer hold such prime position in the theories of causation, though they are still recognised as significant influences in the development and fixation of the pattern for certain neurotic constellations . . .

The way in which a child reacts to any trauma is determined by the total constellation of constitutional trend, his status of physical maturation, his integrative capacity, his previous experiences, and the type of trauma.

Earlier on in this chapter a significant association was noted between older age at placement and perceived unsatisfactory family relationships. This finding pointed to the possible presence of difficulties in the children before placement and perhaps to the failure of the subsequent environmental influences to reverse these earlier traumatic experiences. Obviously the older the child at placement the greater the possibility of it having been exposed to adverse pre-adoption experiences. A variety of other factors may have played their part in bringing about the unhappy experiences related by this group of adoptees. Constitutional inheritance and pre-natal experiences can prejudice a child's capacity to take from his parents in spite of the latters' efforts to give love and affection. It is therefore possible that some adoptees were unable to respond to parental efforts to establish emotional contact with them.

Possible personality difficulties in the parents were another factor which may have contributed to disturbed family relationships. The comments of a number of adoptees indicated that the parents' own unresolved conflicts had a negative influence on them. Whether such difficulties were obvious at placement or appeared later it is difficult to tell. Parents often change as the child grows and their attitudes, feelings and behaviour can vary at different stages of the child's development. Though some of the parents' possible feelings about their infertility could have been triggered off by the adoptive situation, such feelings could not be held directly responsible for most of the difficulties of communication and relationship that the adoptees described. In cases where the parents also had children of their own, the adoptees maintained that emotional sterility and lack of positive experiences were suffered by the parents' natural children too. They added that their parents had as much difficulty in relating to them as they had in relating to their own children. In effect, relationship difficulties mostly appeared to be independent of the adoption situation. One adoptee remarked: 'I cannot say that I was discriminated upon for being adopted because my mother gave no love or affection to her own children by birth.' Another said:

> My brother—that's my parents' own son—and myself had both had psychiatric treatment recently. We were talking the other day and saying how we neither of us felt loved and that our parents seemed unable to show affection. They always seemed to be busy and we rarely saw them at home. Our mother was busy with her Salvation Army activities and our father with his local politics. We used to long for them to talk to us and be with us and take us out to places. . . .

Besides the possibility of personality difficulties in the parents there was that of difficulties arising from the parents' possible feelings about their childlessness, which might have prevented them from emotionally accepting that the child really belonged to them. This could have impaired their capacity to relate to and empathise with the child. If true parenthood, whether intuitive or learned, implies an emotional link-up at the deepest level between the parent and the child, adoptive parents who feel guilty or uncertain about their 'entitlement' to the child may find it difficult to form this link. This is not saying that there is no difference between having an own from having an adopted child, but that for a secure child-parent relationship to be fostered it is necessary for the adoptive parents to come to feel that the child is theirs. Community attitudes or personal considerations may sometimes inhibit parents from being themselves and from responding appropriately. Some adoptees told us of occasions when they overheard neighbours or friends of the family saying to enquirers: 'She is not really theirs, she is only adopted', or, 'He is adopted, you know.' Remarks of this kind may create not only a feeling of 'non-entitlement' in the parents but feelings of not belonging in the child. One adoptee described how her mother was once trying to sympathise with a neighbour whose son was involved in a motor-car accident and in the process she talked about her own distress when her daughter (the adoptee) developed a serious infection and was in hospital for some time. Upon this the neighbour remarked: 'But it cannot be the same; after all she is not your own flesh and blood'. 'My mother', added the adoptee, 'was speechless; she went home and cried . . . it was the first time I saw her so upset and hurt.'

Jaffe and Fanshel,[2] in their recent follow-up study, propound the concept of '*entitlement*' as a useful perspective for understanding the dynamics of adoptive parent behaviour. Whilst, it is argued, the adopted child may be viewed as typically facing the task of resolving complex identity problems with respect to the two sets of parents who have played major roles in his life, the parallel identity challenge facing the adoptive parents is one of developing a feeling of entitlement to this child. Jaffe and Fanshel go on to speculate that whatever hazards exist in adoption from the standpoint of parental behaviour, these were likely to stem from the parents' inability to feel that the adopted children truly belonged to them. It is assumed that the successful resolution of the problem of entitlement signifies that the adoptive mother or father had mastered any basic doubts about his worthiness as a parent, particularly with respect to resolving the psychological 'insult' associated with the problem of infertility. Adoption workers have long assumed that if the individual feels that he or she does not possess true masculinity or femininity because of an inability to procreate, this may well interfere with the development of a sense of parental entitlement to the child and unconscious hostility may be directed towards the adoptee as a symbol of the parents' inability to procreate a child of their own.

Summary

Almost half the adoptees in the sample perceived their adoptive home life as being mostly unsatisfactory and only one in every four described it as satisfactory. They attributed their general unhappiness or dissatisfaction to poor family relationships, lack of close links with their parents and a failure to develop a sense of attachment and belonging. The greater the dissatisfaction with their home life the greater also the possibility that the adoptees would be searching for their original parents. Conversely, the greater the satisfaction with their home life the greater also the possibility that they would be looking for additional background information to 'fill in gaps' or 'tie loose ends'.

Though good relationships were associated with fair to considerable information being made available and poor relationships with none or hostile information, there were also exceptions showing that the withholding of information was not always an indication of insecure relationships. The indications were, however, that a secure and stable relationship made it possible for the adoptive parents to share information without fear and anxiety.

You go out with your girl-friend and you feel you are
nothing; you are only an adopted person and you wonder
what will happen when she finds out. So you try not to tell
and guard it as a secret.

Male adoptee

A number of writers have suggested that adopted children as a
group are particularly prone to display behaviour problems and
symptoms of maladjustment. Beyond the usual causal factors of
maladjustment, adopted children, it is claimed, are subjected to
stress as a result of their adoptive status. Several explanations are
offered, such as the fact that most adopted children are also illegitimate, which in itself has been identified as carrying risks not faced by
children born within wedlock. Also, that the children's mothers
usually experience social and personal problems that may affect
their predisposition during pregnancy and after confinement. The
children themselves often experience separations and pre-adoption
placements that deprive them of the consistent maternal relationship
which is seen as vital in the first months of life. In other words,
whether a constitutional factor is present or not, a deprivation on
the human and environmental side can be decisive in the formation
of an insecure personality. In this context, the quality of the adopted
child's home life can be decisive in furthering its mental health and
reversing earlier depriving and emotionally traumatic experiences.

The evidence, mainly from clinical studies, points to the need to
provide the developing child with essential emotional satisfactions
if a secure and well-founded personality is to emerge. Terms like
firm identity, stable personality or positive self-image are difficult to
define but it is easier perhaps to recognise the person who lacks
these qualities and feels the impoverishment of human ties, the inability to love and to relate, or the fear of isolation and being cut off.

The origins of identity are traced, by some writers, back to the
very early experiences of the baby while he is still in the womb and
soon afterwards. The sense of self itself, it is claimed, originates in
the body. The baby needs a lot of sensory input, that is it has to be

stimulated, and to be mothered. The mother supplies this through warmth and play and helps to build up a feeling of self inside the baby. If the feeding and other experiences go well, the child grows a kind of good central self and the feeling of goodness begins to develop within him. At first the baby has no awareness of others but as its resources grow, usually by the second half of the first year, it develops the capacity to tell when something is inside or outside. At the end of the first year, some writers claim, most babies have a definite personality. If the child's emotional hunger or his impetus to grow and become a separate individual are not met, it can cause feelings of vacuum, of being unloved and unwanted, and a shrinking of the self inside. Such people never feel real and are not committed to anything. Later development, it is argued, is founded on this first year. It is acknowledged, however, that the quality of subsequent experiences or the strength of possible stress may affect adversely even well-adjusted individuals. The extent and duration, however, of the psychological upset would be expected to reflect the intensity of the current stress and of the former coping capacity of the individual.

Apart from the importance of the mother-child relationship at first, identity appears to be a compound of other multiple family, personal and socio-cultural influences. Evidence suggests that it is the quality of such influences and relationships that determines, to a large extent, the kind of personality an individual develops. A sense of self-image, bodily and mental, is cultivated from the moment the young infant begins to recognise another face, to gradual identification and assimilation of other confirmatory experiences about his own parents, his ancestors, his people, his country and its history. The type of personal relationships a person develops, first with the family and later outside, the values, traditions and standards of the culture which are transmitted through the family to the individual member is the material on which identities are based. In other words the 'I' of the present is an accumulation of all the 'I's of yesterday and yesteryear and can only be understood in the context of family relationships, relatives, origins, environment, culture etc. Families and societies also assign roles and tasks to individuals within which they can recognise themselves and feel they belong. All these experiences are interrelated by the growing individual and eventually form the core of his identity. The ability to cope satisfactorily with different life situations or to enter into relationships with others, is largely dependent on the strength and quality of the individual's identity. The opposite of this core of identity is a sense of 'isolation,' 'vacuum' or 'emptiness'.

It is for reasons quoted above that adopted children, apart from good nurturing experiences, also need to have information about their biological and sociological background to help them complete their self-image. Obviously where the remaining parts of identity are negative, no amount of background information is likely to rectify this. In the previous chapters we saw how most adoptees came to know late about their adoptions and how they were given no or very little information about their forebears; and, also, that the great majority perceived their adoptions as unsatisfactory or only as partly satisfactory. The combination of all these experiences would, on the outset, suggest that many of these adoptees would have developed negative identities fraught with anxieties and insecurities.

Self-image and adjustment

Adoptees in the sample were ready to talk about themselves, their preoccupations and pressures. They also talked about their adoptive status and its significance to them. They described some of their inner feelings and thoughts and tried to put across a picture of how they perceived themselves. They talked about their relationships, their anxieties, insecurities and their current life situations trying to help the writer to understand their position. They generally talked of the kind of person they saw themselves to be and of their self-image. The way they described themselves conveyed a picture of their sense of personal identity.

Adjustment in life is a very nebulous and difficult thing to define or assess. The assessment of personality and of the way people cope with life situations can be open to many subjective interpretations. The same applies to concepts about maturity or stability. Factors that need to be considered range from psycho-social to socio-cultural and socio-economic and these are difficult to define or, even worse, to isolate and measure. Available personality and other tests are noted more for their bias and unreliability rather than for their accuracy.

Because of the difficulties outlined, it was thought more appropriate to classify 'adjustment' by relying on the adoptees' own account of how they perceived themselves and how settled they felt. One other method we could have followed was to group separately adoptees who had psychiatric treatment. Though reference is made to this group later in this chapter, such classification would again have serious drawbacks because of the observation made during the study that the boundary line between those who had psychiatric treatment and many of the rest was a very thin one. It was mostly accidental, for instance, that some adoptees in the non-psychiatric group had not received such help yet. The general picture gained from the majority of adoptees searching for their origins was one of unhappiness and inner pressures and worries making coping with life situations a great effort.

Most of the adoptees had a story or experience to relate which they thought was unique to themselves. Experiences such as the way they were told or found out about their adoption and about their home situations assumed considerable emotional proportions which had been preoccupying them for a long time. They shared what they felt were important and often painful experiences to themselves.

One group of forty-four adoptees (or 65 per cent) perceived themselves in what appeared to be negative or fairly negative terms and with a poor self-image. They saw themselves as unhappy, were generally troubled about their relationships and about their adoptive status and its implications. With the remaining twenty-four adoptees such feelings were either absent or of less intensity and balanced by equally good feelings about themselves. Those who felt troubled and unhappy talked about experiencing a sense of 'emptiness', 'isolation' or 'vacuum'; of feeling 'false', 'not being a whole or a real person', 'depressed and unhappy', 'tense and anxious', 'not coping', 'unable to get close to people'. The rest either did not express such feelings or if they did there was less intensity and urgency behind them, compared with the first group. They were generally less troubled about their adoptive status or about their illegitimacy and appeared to be coping better with current life situations, such as work and family. The adoptees who were placed for adoption when a year old or more were significantly in the group that put across a negative self-perception.

When the adoptees' perception of themselves was related to their views about the quality of their family relationships, an interesting picture emerged which showed the close connection between the two (see Appendix: Table 6.1). Of thirty-one adoptees who perceived their adoption as unsatisfactory, twenty-eight also referred to themselves as 'unhappy' or 'depressed and anxious' and generally conveyed a negative self-image. At the other end, of eighteen adoptees who saw their adoptions as mainly satisfactory, only three described themselves as 'confused' or 'anxious' or 'depressed' or unable to cope with current life situations. In general, there was a close association between the adoptees' perception of themselves and their perception of their family relationships. Those who felt they had a rather unhappy home life also felt unsettled and insecure, whilst those who felt they had a reasonably satisfactory home life generally felt happier and under less pressure from within.

Of the forty-four adoptees whose concept of themselves appeared negative or fairly negative and who portrayed a poor self-image, almost four out of every five were now looking for their original parents (see Appendix: Table 6.2); in contrast, of the twenty-four adoptees who described themselves in terms implying better adjustment, only one out of every three were searching for their original parents whilst the rest were only interested in background information.

Age at placement and self-perception   Of sixteen adoptees placed when one year or older, thirteen portrayed a very negative self-image with strong feelings of isolation, uncertainty and insecurity.

Psychiatric help   Almost two out of every five adoptees in the sample had received psychiatric help at some stage in their lives or were still under treatment. As stated earlier, it was accidental that some other adoptees who were labouring under similar preoccupations and inner pressures had not had such help. The conditions from which the psychiatric group suffered ranged from serious psychotic breakdowns to various forms of depression and anxiety states. Though a slightly higher percentage of adoptees who were brought up as only children appeared in the psychiatric group the difference between them and those brought up with siblings was not statistically significant. However, there were indications that adoptees brought up as only children were more vulnerable compared with the rest. (The presence or absence of older or younger siblings within the adoptive home was not connected with the adoptees having had psychiatric treatment.)

A very high percentage of those in the psychiatric group perceived their adoptive home life as unsatisfactory and only one adoptee was positive about the outcome of his adoption (see Appendix: Table

6.3). Four out of every five of the adoptees in the psychiatric group were now searching for their original parents.

Twelve of the sixteen children who were placed when a year or older featured in the psychiatric group and two more asked to be put in touch with psychiatric help.

The general picture

The general picture that emerged from an examination of the adoptees' self-perception was that those who portrayed a negative, non-adjustive picture of themselves, perceived their adoptive home life as depriving, they were mostly searching for their birth-parents; and they were given no information or only negative type of information about their origins. Being placed at a year or older seemed to carry considerable risks.

HOW ADOPTEES SEARCHING FOR THEIR ORIGINAL PARENTS
PERCEIVED THEMSELVES

As stated earlier, two out of every three adoptees felt unsettled, unhappy or under considerable inner pressure. They mainly attributed this to the fact of being adopted and to the poor quality of their home life and family relationships. It was also found that the greater the pressure from within the greater the possibility that the adoptees would be searching for their first parents; where the pressure was less or induced from outside—i.e., newspaper publicity—it was more likely that they would be looking for background information, sometimes additional to what they already knew. The views of Mrs Crammond were typical of how adoptees who were searching for their parents perceived themselves:

— You look at yourself in the mirror and you can't compare it with anybody. You're a stranger because you don't know what your real mother looks like or what your father looks like . . . You can't turn round and say I look like my mother or I look like my father. You can't do that because you don't know what they look like. I am a stranger to myself. You must know who your people were and what they looked like. I felt humble when they told me I was adopted at the age of fifteen. I had just known my husband then and I felt that to be adopted was dreadful. An adopted person you know! I was never happy and I never felt

I fitted in with my family . . . I was very insecure . . . never
fitted in. Being adopted makes me feel so strongly that if ever
I had a baby out of wedlock I wouldn't have it adopted, you
have this obsession about being adopted . . . or the child
perhaps should never be able to know it was adopted and such
feelings would then never arise.

Mrs McLure, now in her mid-thirties and who had earlier talked
of her unhappy relationship with her mother, described herself as
someone with 'no true identity' and 'not knowing who I am'. She
then went on:

All through my life I had the feeling of unreality about myself;
a feeling of not being real, something like an imitation antique
. . . I have been told that I was born in the Poor House and
that my birth-mother was a bad lot. This has been haunting me.
I tried desperately to avoid being like her but then who am I
like? I feel I have nothing to pass onto my children and this
bothers me. It is a strange thing to say but I feel I cannot make
contact with people . . .

A fairly successful self-employed adoptee described feelings of
'emptiness' and 'isolation' which made him feel miserable. At the
time of the interview he was on tranquillisers from his family doctor
and complained of finding little pleasure in life:

I am like an island and I feel I have nobody. I find it difficult
to show my feelings to my children and when at the pub I feel
like a stranger to everybody and want to retreat. I think there is
something about adoption that gives you a feeling of insecurity
as regards just exactly who you are, or what exactly love is.
You read about the sense of loss people experience when they
lose somebody but when my father died I didn't feel it as a loss
and it didn't seem to affect me. This bothered me and I kept
wondering if my adoption made me different from other people . . .

Mr Proctor found out about his adoption when he was nineteen.
By then he was already feeling suicidal and depressed and after the
revelation he had to go into hospital. The revelation of adoption
appeared to be the final stress to an already precariously coping
person. Another adoptee, Miss Bell, was feeling very unhappy and
confused at the time of the interview. She was then planning to

G

emigrate to Canada hoping she would become a 'new person'. She 'hated' herself, felt 'not likeable', 'isolated' and 'unable to mix or make friends'. She described her adoption as disastrous and saw her difficulties as resulting from the type of upbringing she had. She felt rejected by everybody and believed that 'as an adopted person you do not have much status'. She placed her own illegitimate child for adoption because she found it difficult to respond to it. She would have liked to keep it but she was aware of her limitations: 'Perhaps this is what my mother was feeling before she gave me up. I am trying through my own experience to understand what my mother felt at the time. This was something I wondered about since I found out at the age of eleven.'

A girl who recently dropped out of university was at odds with her family and feeling hopeless. She had been taking drugs and wanted advice about possible help. She knew she was adopted since early childhood but she maintained that she had few satisfying experiences. She was very critical and bitter, attributing her 'unhappiness' and 'depriving' experiences to her adoption: 'I feel funny and not whole. I am unable to experience things and I cannot relate emotionally to people. It feels like you not being you and that what is you is thoroughly bad . . . there should be no adoption. Preferable for all girls to be aborted'.

Later she questioned how far she felt like this because she was adopted or because of her poor relationships at home. A young female adoptee who found out about her adoption at eleven remarked:

> For a long time the business of who I am, what I am and so forth has been on my mind. I feel very unsettled and I changed several trainings before this one. I was finding it very difficult to accept the reality of life. I was bothered by the fact of my adoption and still am. I feel as being only half a person, the other half being obscured by my adoption. I always had this bout of stomach troubles and the doctors could find nothing wrong . . . I then had to go into a psychiatric clinic.

Mrs Hendry found out about her adoption when she was studying to become a teacher. Now at twenty-six she felt she could not postpone trying to find her first mother. At the time of the interview she was feeling very desolate and depressed and was critical of her professional parents for having been rigid and demanding. Reflecting on her present situation she remarked:

> I feel I am a person not in my own right. I feel I have lived a lie . . . I stand before the mirror and ask, 'Who am I? Who do I belong to?' There are times when I wish I had not been born . . . I feel I need a whole new life, as if everything has been a huge deception. Soon after I found I was adopted I realised that adopted people are a race apart. When I told my fiancé his reaction was, 'I do not know what my father and mother will feel.' You see his mother was very family-tree conscious and very class-conscious too. When my boy was born and my mother-in-law visited me in hospital she exclaimed: 'Thank God he has taken from our side of the family.' I know what she was getting at and it hurt.

Why some adoptees felt no embarrassment at being adopted whilst others were very conscious of it is difficult to say. The possible explanation is that such a perception must be dependent on the adoptee's general image of himself and how positive this is to be able to cope with the facts of the adoptive status. Obviously the environment—including the parents—can reinforce a good or poor image about adoption depending on circumstances. The community itself, as stated previously, may look upon adoption as a second best and that being adopted carries some element of stigma. After all, it is only in the last twenty or thirty years that adoption stopped being regarded as occurring only among the lower classes. Remnants of such attitudes appear still to influence both parents and children. Adoptees talked of feeling 'embarrassed' or of being 'bothered' or 'worried' about being adopted. 'You are one of a minority,' one of them said, 'and when people hear you are adopted they expect you to be different.' One adoptee said that when she was about to marry and still not knowing of her adoptive status, a neighbour met her fiancé and said: 'I think it is proper to warn you that this girl is adopted; my husband told me about it only recently.'

Another young adoptee was apprehensive about telling his fiancée that he was adopted: 'You never know how she is going to take it. There is a lot of stigma in being adopted because you are also illegitimate. When I hear the word bastard I feel like hitting out . . . I am now beginning to take things a bit more easily.'

'You are ashamed to tell your girl-friend that you are an adopted child . . .,' said Mr Proctor, 'it is like not being a proper person and you feel humble.' A married woman also remarked:

> When your boy-friend takes you to his people and even after you marry, they keep asking you, 'Where were you born, who are your parents?' It is dreadful to have to tell them you do not know and that you are adopted. When they hear you're adopted they think there is something wrong with you.

From relatives' comments Mrs Drummond confirmed in her own mind that being adopted was seen by some people as being 'different':

> My niece who is now seventeen was not getting on well with her mother and she was being very difficult. I told her mother that at this stage most children are like this and that I myself couldn't speak to my mother at that age. Her reply was: 'You were different. She was not your mother; you were only adopted.' This really hit me very hard. It brought it home to me that I was adopted and perhaps different.

Though Mrs McVicar learned about her adoption twelve years ago when she was twenty-two, she attributed it to her adoption for feeling 'different', 'empty and isolated' or 'not like other people'.

> You feel you have no family like everybody else. What you call family is not really yours and the relatives are not your relatives . . . there was always a gap between me and my parents and I feel such a gap in myself now. Being adopted must make you feel like that.

Like some other adoptees, Mrs McVicar felt that her inability to form real relationships was connected with her parents' difficulty to relate to her because she was an adopted child to them.

Mrs Thomas didn't know either that she was adopted until she was twenty. Ever since, she has been feeling that she is 'nobody' and with 'no identity at all'.

> People say you are like your father and you build yourself on this and suddenly you feel this is not so . . . In a way, when I discovered I was adopted it was a relief to me because of the situation between my father and my mother. The thing is that I don't feel I know who I am and it is a feeling I had when I was younger and if I live to be ninety it will bother me and be

the same . . . just the fact that you don't know who you are stays with you for life. It is a weird thing . . . I still feel I have no identity. I don't think anybody can appreciate it when they have not experienced this vacuum . . . My husband is a bit funny about me being adopted—he is not all that keen. I think it is because his background is so stable.

In the case of both Mrs McVicar and Mrs Thomas, though the adoption revelation came very late and was experienced as shattering, both described earlier experiences within their families which indicated poor and unsatisfactory relationships in their formative years. The crisis of revelation appeared to play into earlier insecurities and had been continuing since then. Mrs McSweeney also learned about her adoption late when she was nineteen and she thought that finding she was adopted added to her already considerable difficulties in relationships. At the same time she could see how she focused a lot of her anxieties on a preoccupation with her adoptive status:

I never really felt that I belonged. I find it difficult to make friends or be close to people and for this I blame partly my upbringing. For a couple of years I hovered on the edge of a breakdown . . . I was on phenobarbitones for some time . . . I have always been feeling inferior. I know that my fiancé's father wasn't told about my adoption because he wouldn't have approved. When he found out he wasn't very pleased but there wasn't very much he could do . . . Being adopted means you are illegitimate, 'bad blood' and all that kind of thing . . . I couldn't bear to hear the word bastard for a long time . . . I was pregnant myself before being married and this just crowned it as far as my mother and father's family were concerned—this was my 'bad blood' coming out—the fact that I had to get married and I was illegitimate myself. They will probably be watching poor Gill—my daughter—when she is that age to see if she is displaying the same tendencies . . .

HOW ADOPTEES IN SEARCH OF BACKGROUND INFORMATION
PERCEIVED THEMSELVES

Adoptees in this group generally had a more positive self-image compared with those searching for their parents; they described themselves as 'fairly contented' people, they were less 'bothered' by

89

their adoptive status or by their illegitimacy, they were under less pressure from within and their family relationships were predominantly more satisfactory. A secretary, who found out at the age of eleven, remarked that being adopted never posed any problems to her at any time:

> It never stood in my way. My adoption does not bother me and perhaps this is because I was made by my parents to feel that I was not different from my brother [their own son]. It made no difference learning about my adoption when I was ten or eleven. I see myself as a contented person but now that my parents are dead I would like to find out a bit more about my birth-mother. My adoptive parents knew very little to tell me.

Another adoptee whose parents told him everything that they knew about his origins was hoping to find out more from his search. He described himself as a 'fairly happy' person, who had a 'good home'. He does not think he is different from other people and he has a wide circle of friends and acquaintances. He never felt the lack of a blood-tie and he would not have wished things to have been different:

> I felt a bit different when I was an adolescent and I didn't know whether it was because I was adopted. I then wondered if I were the odd one out. For a short while it was worrying because I didn't know whether what I was experiencing, especially as regards sex, was normal. I had nothing by which to compare my experience. I felt a bit on my own then. But my family were good to me at the time when I was a bit difficult and that period was for me one of self-discovery. I think I discovered myself and my family at that stage . . . mixing with other lads also helped me to understand that my feelings were not strange. I think that all these experiences helped me to adjust.

Mr Newsom's perception of himself was of a confident and secure young man. 'I don't see myself as being any different from anybody else . . . Being adopted has never bothered me . . . I realise that most adopted children are illegitimate but it really doesn't bother me. I had good parents who made me feel secure and that I mattered'.

Similar feelings were expressed by Mrs Scott who only found out about her adoption at the age of eighteen:

90

I am generally a contented person . . . My adoption does not bother me in the least though sometimes I wonder why I was given up . . . I enjoy my home life and the question of who I am does not preoccupy my mind. The fact of illegitimacy is something I understood in my early teens but somehow it did not bother me . . . if you don't feel something it is difficult to explain it . . . My adoptive parents were my father and mother and I did not see that illegitimacy referred to me . . .

Though adoptees who perceived themselves in negative terms were generally upset when they realised that adoption and illegitimacy were closely connected, those with a better image of themselves seemed to be less bothered: 'I rarely look upon myself as illegitimate', said some in this latter group, and another: 'There is nothing wrong in being adopted. When I first met my wife I told her that I was adopted and she said, "It doesn't make any difference like," and this made me feel even better, it never really bothered me.'

Summary

The majority of adoptees searching for their origins conveyed a picture of alienations and poor self-image which they generally attributed to depriving experiences within the adoptive home. A considerable number of these had received psychiatric treatment to help them cope with life situations. They expressed feelings of shame and embarrassment about their adoptive status and the implied illegitimacy. The greater their sense of isolation and insecurity the greater the possibility they would be searching for their original parents. A search for more background information was generally associated with a better self-image and a more satisfactory home life.

Since my parents died I have been feeling rootless and lonely;
I have nowhere to turn to. I do not belong. My parents had
no relatives and they relied too much on each other . . .
something I feel is missing from my life. I must now know
about my blood relations and find my birth-mother . . . I
wouldn't perhaps feel like this if my parents were alive, but this
has become very important for me now, too important to stop.
                                                    Male adoptee

The step of enquiring and searching was not taken lightly by most
adoptees. The final step usually came at the end of a fair amount of
deliberation and usually at a stage when 'it could not be put off any
longer'. The suggestion was that inner pressures, often increased by
outside crises or events, eventually moved the adoptee in this direction. Both groups of adoptees—the Meet the Natural Parents and
the Background Information ones—appeared to experience these
pressures in various degrees though those in the first group felt a
greater urgency compared with the rest.

Most adoptees had at some point previously thought of searching
into their origins and genealogy. The first time that they had considered doing this had generally been in adolescence but they took
no action for a long time. Only four of the forty-nine adoptees, who
came to know that they were adopted before the age of seventeen,
took actual steps to find information when they reached the age at
which they were entitled by law to obtain it. All four knew that they
were adopted before they reached the age of ten. Other adoptees
who entertained such wishes took action only at a later stage when
the desire reappeared with greater intensity. For instance, of fifteen
adoptees who were told or found out about their adoption between
the ages of thirteen and seventeen, none tried to search on reaching
the age of seventeen—as allowed by the law—but the actual step
was taken three to ten years later. This did not mean that they had
not thought of doing so, but once the turmoil of adolescence was
over the need seemed to abate. Though sudden revelation in

adolescence or an unsatisfactory home life generated at the time a desire to find the first set of parents, the adoptees did not act upon it. Some felt that they might not have been able to control the situation if they had tried to do so in their teens. The eventual search was the result of a combination of experiences and feelings from the past as well as from current life situations. At this stage, need or fantasy intensified by current events became urgent and could not be postponed. A girl who waited till she was twenty-two before trying to find out remarked:

> I knew I was adopted since I was four or five but it was about the age of twelve that I started wondering who my parents were. Then my parents sent me to a boarding school and I was so upset that I used to tell myself that my real parents wouldn't have done this to me . . . I then thought about enquiring when I was sixteen, but I put it off. Why now? Perhaps I feel more lonely; I had a tiff with my boy friend recently and he has left . . . My parents I don't get on with.

'It has been at the back of my mind to find my natural parents for a few years now', said a thirty-year-old policeman, who came to know accidentally of his adoption at the age of thirteen (his parents never acknowledged the fact):

> I now feel that I cannot postpone it any more. My brother, who was the only person close to me, died recently and this has made up my mind. I feel I have nobody . . . I must do something and find out. If my mother and father had told me about this at ten or eleven or even younger, I might have forgotten all about it—but all this secrecy and no trusting has made me wonder more and more; but it is my brother's death that has really decided me.

Another adoptee who had a stormy adolescence felt he had to find his other parents as they might 'understand' him better. Yet at seventeen he decided against it and left the search till he was twenty-five: 'I couldn't do it then: I was so immature and I was afraid I would be unable to manage it . . . why now? We are about to have our first child; you wonder about yourself and the kind of parent that puts out a child for adoption'.

Among adoptees who were 'feeling unhappy or generally dissatisfied', the tendency was to wait till after marriage before embarking on a search for the natural parents. There was a hope that marriage

would bring satisfactions that would make finding the original
parents unnecessary:

> There are times when you feel unloved and unhappy and wonder
> what it is like to be with your real parents. You wonder what
> you have missed not being with them. But you comfort yourself
> and say: Wait until you marry and have a family of your own
> and have people to love and to love you . . . it will be different
> you tell yourself. But I am married now three years and it is
> not any different. I still have the same feelings of emptiness . . .

Other adoptees who placed high expectations on their marriages
were disappointed to find that some of their personal needs and
pressures continued to be with them: 'I thought that once married I
would forget and things would be better but I soon started wondering
and worrying again. Marriage did not make me feel any different'.

The original causes giving rise to the wish to search appeared to
date from different stages in the adoptees' life, especially before they
reached their late teens. The wish to search could have been there
since adolescence but it was translated into action at some later
stage when some kind of crisis upset traditional or precarious ways
of coping. Non-adopted people faced with a crisis which threatens
their functioning may resort to psychiatrists, social workers, or their
family doctors, but the adopted person has a choice: he may either
resort to the same caring agencies in the community or connect his
difficulties with his adoptive status and cherish the hope that tracing
his origins will bring about the desired relief.

Before finally writing to or calling at Register House most adoptees
experienced further doubts, fears or anxieties about the wisdom of
their act. The fear was of hurting either themselves or others in the
process. One adoptee remarked: 'I had been thinking of finding out
more for the last few years but I could not bring myself to do so.
It is like an X-ray; I was afraid of what I would find.' Another one
went outside Register House on three different occasions before he
could bring himself to go in: 'I didn't want to do any damage to
anyone else. I thought if I started digging up things somebody
might be hurt; it could be me, it could be somebody else; in the end
I couldn't leave it any longer and I simply had to find out.' Others
remarked how they often came to Edinburgh—where Register House
is—and though they had thought of enquiring it was only now that
they felt a real urge to do so:

I came to Edinburgh from London at least three times before I could bring myself to ask. Why this time? I was feeling more depressed and empty; I was given your letter at the same time I enquired and my reaction was to do nothing about it; but I felt so miserable afterwards that I wanted to talk to somebody and this is how I 'phoned you earlier . . .

Mr Barrow, a professional person, remarked about his actual step: 'When inside the building I never felt so nervous in my life; I felt like running away but then I said, "It was either now or never." ' The mixed feelings of other adoptees about the search were expressed in such comments as, 'you want to do it and you don't', or 'you feel always in two minds until something happens and that decides you to go and find out.' Mr Stanton was toying with the idea for some time:

Once I almost posted a letter to Register House and then decided to forget about it; but this is not something you can forget. At first I thought this would push me back and all that and better not bother about it, but recently the urge to straighten myself has become very strong again and I decided to act . . .

The promptings of a wife or husband—who sometimes appeared more curious than the adoptee—influenced a small number of them to act a bit prematurely by their reckoning: 'My wife keeps saying, "Do you never wonder like?" . . .' 'She has been pushing me a bit', or, 'My wife has been on at me for some time, "Why don't you do something about it? What sort of person are you who does not want to find out about his real parents?" I think she is more curious than I am'. One husband, who was told about his wife's adoption by her parents, held it back from her for five years. When the fact came out, he was dealing with his guilt by urging her to find her original mother. The husband of another adoptee was showing his hostility towards his wife by spending considerable time trying to trace his genealogy and taunting her for not even knowing who her real mother or father were: 'It makes you want to prove to him who you are,' said the wife.

Only eight of the seventy adoptees seemed to be unconcerned about the possible effect of their search on their adoptive parents. It was the wish of the rest to avoid doing anything that might upset or hurt their feelings. They mostly tried to carry out their enquiries discreetly and, with the exception of two, the rest were careful not to let their adoptive parents know. (Because in a great number of cases one or both parents were already dead, this kind of consideration did not often present itself.) They stressed that, irrespective of the reasons for their search, and of the expectations from it, their primary loyalties were to their adoptive parents: 'They are the only people I know'; or, 'I would never dream of doing anything that might hurt them'; or, 'the only people that matter are the ones who bring you up but when these are gone . . .'. When thinking of parents or of father or mother, the people that automatically came to mind were their adoptive parents and not some imaginary set of parents. Such feelings, with the exception noted earlier of those whose unhappiness reached extreme proportions, were held irrespective of the quality of the relationship between the adoptee and his family. Where relationships had been very poor and where secrecy and evasiveness prevailed, the adoptees were sad and very critical, but still retained considerable feelings for the people who brought them up. They would refer to their birth-parents as mother or father but only the mention of their adoptive parents evoked an emotional response.

Normative or other crises which made the search necessary now

Most adoptees experienced an intense impulse to search for their origins because of a crisis or event which appeared to give rise to certain intense emotions and reactions. As all adoptees who face similar crises do not react in the same way, it must be assumed that those who search are more vulnerable. In other words, the crisis itself was not enough to explain the intense needs displayed but often it triggered them off. Crises, some normative and others not, which finally set the adoptees on their search, were mainly connected with such events as death of a parent, separation or divorce, marriage, child-birth, adolescence, and middle age. Sometimes more than one such crisis combined to make the need for the search appear urgent.

In both the Meet the Natural Parents group and the Background Information group the decisive factor for the recent research was usually a crisis in the adoptee's life. The only difference between the two groups was in the reaction to the crisis. The Background Information group seemed to be less threatened by the crisis and they reacted in a more adjustive way. In contrast, the Meet the Natural Parents group reacted with more apparent stress and anxiety.

The crisis seemed to pose for them a real threat to their hitherto coping abilities.

Death of a parent

The crisis of bereavement featured considerably in this sample of seventy adoptees. How far it also features to the same extent in the lives of non-adopted people or other adopted people it is not possible to say. The effect on the adoptees and the feelings that it triggered were, however, unmistakable. Forty adoptees (or three out of every five) connected their search with the loss of one or both parents which had happened at some earlier stage. For sixteen of them the loss occurred before they were fifteen. In three of the latter cases both parents died before the adoptee was fifteen. Parental loss through death featured almost in equal percentages in both the Find the Natural Parent group and the Background Information one.

Whether the death of a parent happened before or after adolescence, it usually left adoptees with feelings of loss, abandonment and distress. Where the relationship with the deceased parent had not been very good, there was a mixture of guilt and anger. One adoptee, who lost one parent before the age of fifteen and the other not long after, talked of having nobody to turn to and of feeling 'in a void, empty and nothing'; another felt 'lost and lonely': A young woman who lost both her parents before she was fourteen felt desolate and abandoned:

> After my father died I realised that the family obviously weren't going to have me and my sister, and we were farmed out from one hostel to another and I knew that I was abandoned and I didn't really have a home any more. I didn't have someone I could associate myself with and it was then I think that I started to wonder just who my real mother was. I wanted somebody to belong. Before I always had somebody. I knew I couldn't find out about my birth-mother because I was not seventeen yet. Well, my seventeenth birthday was on a Sunday and I couldn't do it on the Monday and on the Tuesday I had to work, so on the Wednesday I came down to Register House . . .

Mr Simpson, though critical of his mother for not disclosing his adoption to him early, had a very close relationship with her and, when she died, felt 'utterly lost'. He remarked:

> I was sixteen at the time and I felt I had no one to turn to;
> I mean if I had any problems I could turn to my mother and
> get advice from her, but once she was gone I couldn't bring
> myself to ask my brother or sister and I couldn't ask my father
> because he just half the time didn't understand what I was
> getting on about. She was a great loss to me. She was the
> guiding hand at the time, so I just felt empty . . . If my mother
> had lived it wouldn't have been necessary to do this. But now
> there's only one person who can give me the answers I need
> and that's my mother through birth. That's the only one.

Time and again many of these adoptees said that they would not have embarked on their search if one or both parents were alive. This they felt 'wouldn't be fair on them', or 'I wouldn't dream of doing this'; or even 'there wouldn't be any need'. 'It must have been on my mind to search,' said a young married man, 'but I couldn't hurt my mother; when she went to her grave I felt there was no one to hurt and I was certain then that I simply *had* to find out who my original mother was.'

A young professional woman, who was searching for more information about her background would never have done so, she said, if her widowed 'mother' were still alive:

> When she died I felt slightly more out on a limb as it were . . .
> one did feel a bit alone as if abandoned; I just felt more
> rootless—I suppose that is what made me try and find out more
> about my background. I also thought it would be disloyal to
> her if I had tried before; I wouldn't have liked her to know
> that I was trying as it might upset her. No, the truth is I
> didn't really feel the same need before she died.

Mrs Drummond felt 'lonely and friendless' when her father died and her mother re-married not long after. She could hardly contain the bitterness felt at her mother's re-marriage. She is now hoping to gain a lot of satisfaction through meeting her birth-mother. Another adoptee was twenty when her parents died. She then felt an intense impulse to find out who her first parents were: 'So when they died I came up to Edinburgh to enquire . . . I felt then I had to find them . . . I didn't care who they were or what they were'.

There was no doubt that parental loss, at whatever stage it

happened, left many adoptees feeling 'lonely', 'lost', 'abandoned', 'rootless' or 'depressed'. The death seemed to give them the feeling of a second loss and further abandonment, viewing the surrender by the natural mother as the original one. Irrespective of the quality of their home life, the adoptees experienced the surrender by the natural mother as a rejection. Where family relationships were positive and strong this trauma seemed to heal, but it was re-opened again at the loss of the adoptive parents. The group who had a more generally satisfying home life seemed to cope better with the loss compared with the rest of the adoptees. Where family relationships had not been experienced as satisfactory and the death of one or both parents occurred, the adoptees expressed strong feelings not only of 'abandonment' but also of 'anger' towards the parents for not giving them enough to cope with life. The trauma of the original 'rejection' seemed to re-appear in an intense form which set these latter adoptees on the way to find the original parents.

A further indication of the adoptees' strong reaction to parental loss and rejection was observed, as illustrated earlier, in cases where the surviving parent re-married soon afterwards. All such adoptees were very critical and angry with the re-marrying parent. They felt pushed out and spoke of their parents' 'lack of interest' in them or in their children; 'not concerned about me any more'; 'I mean nothing to her'; 'I now have nobody.' All were set on meeting their natural parent(s) as the only person left to turn to.

Giving birth to an own child

In eleven cases the adoptees' need to search and find out more about themselves and their background seemed to be motivated by the expectation of an own child and, in two cases, of an adopted child. Mostly female adoptees, but also two males, made a connection between their current search and the coming child. The coming child seemed to re-awaken in them an earnest desire to know more about themselves in preparation for the experience of parenthood. They also seemed to be trying to understand their natural parents' feelings at the time they were having them and especially when they were surrendering them: 'My curiosity and urgency to find out about my mother reached a decisive point when I was expecting my own child. It was a curious feeling but I suddenly wanted to find out about my mother, why she gave me up, what she felt at the time'.

99

Another woman added: 'For the first time in my life I had flesh and blood of my own; it was then I felt this in me that I wanted to trace my mother.' The urge to find her mother started for Mrs King at the time she, too, was expecting her first child: 'I suddenly felt that something was missing from my life and that I had to find my mother. I'm not one who can get close to people and at this time I felt I needed somebody badly. My adopted mother never made me feel I could confide to her.'

From the moment Mr Erickson was told by his wife that they were to have their first baby, his mind was preoccupied with questions about his origins, his first mother and why she surrendered him:

Why children are put up for adoption and why unwanted? You should know the reason why; I've had a reasonable life myself but the thought of another life is intriguing like; it kind of draws you out, pulls you towards it . . . and you ask, 'Why adoption, why?' . . . this is a big stumbling block in adoption. So I feel I must find out. Find out from my mother herself.

Mr Davidson married five years ago and because he and his wife could not have children they applied to adopt. A child was about to be placed with them at the time of the search:

My interest to find out more about my background has suddenly been stimulated by the idea of having a child, an adoptee like myself. I have no blood relations and my adopted child will have none. It will all be rather unconnected . . . but I feel it is important to find out now where I fit in and where my child is going to fit in.

A single woman, who recently gave up her newly born child, was dealing with her feelings of guilt and depression by saying, among other things, that she would welcome him if in adult life he wanted to get in touch with her. She thought that if she could feel like this for her own child, her original mother must be feeling the same about her and therefore would welcome the opportunity to meet her.

Marriage/separation/divorce

Impending marriage, a recent divorce, a broken engagement or loss of a boy- or girl-friend, featured as other happenings which appeared to trigger off a desire to search for the original parents or find out more about themselves. In this, as in other cases, loss or disappointment generated an inward, self-examining tendency and a preoccupation with their origins. Perhaps for adoptees, unlike others, this is the most convenient focus for nagging feelings. The prospect also of marriage, the responsibilities involved, having own children or the disappointment from a failure in marriage or friendship tended to give rise to a need for outside nourishment or for information about their origins. There were features in all these situations which indicated that the adoptees' own insecurity, their lack of a more firm identity or the paucity of their inner resources to cope with a 'rejection' or disappointment or new responsibilities were underlying the quest for the search.

One adoptee in his mid-twenties who saw himself as different and who felt he was 'nothing', changed his wedding plans and went to Register House to enquire about his origins. When he saw the writer he expressed many mixed feelings about his coming marriage and great uncertainty about his ability to shoulder family responsibilities. He blamed his home life and his adoption for his insecurities and hoped that learning about his origins and meeting his natural mother would resolve some of his difficulties and increase his confidence.

Another young man had been wanting to find out more about his natural parents but kept putting it off for the last three to four years. It was only recently when he was jilted by his girl-friend that he suddenly felt he had to find his birth-mother. He was at odds with his adoptive parents and he felt that his original mother was the only one who could help him in his present state of mind. As he appeared fairly depressed and suicidal at the time of the interview he was put in touch with appropriate help.

Miss Spears, who talked with deep feeling about her attachment to her adoptive father, was also greatly troubled by the fact of two broken engagements. She thought that this might be connected with the fact of her adoption, disregarding the fact that broken engagements happen also to non-adopted people:

> I have been engaged twice and I have broken it off; I do not
> know why; I cannot explain it and I do not know where my
> adoption ties up . . . I cannot see why my adoption should make
> me feel an aversion to men . . . you then begin to wonder
> about the kind of person your first mother was . . .

H

Attributing such happenings to adoption possibly provides some relief for the adoptee who can at the same time feel that it is something she can do nothing about.

The crisis of adolescence

Sixteen of the adoptees (or 23 per cent) were told or, as in most instances, found out about their adoption between the ages of thirteen and seventeen. Adolescence is the stage described by psychologists and child development experts as the period when the individual undergoes a deep emotional turmoil, with the search for self-identity revolving, among other things, around one's parents and forebears. The adolescent is seen as an individual who is unsure of himself, of his sexual and vocational role, and of the expectations of society. Adolescence is also traditionally the age of hero-worship, of identification with what is seen as a greater and more complete personality, which has resolved all the doubts of the adolescent. The turmoil, which the adolescent experiences, is part of a normal developmental phase whose positive outcome usually is a more definite and firm identity. Many writers further maintain that where the individual has experienced good relationships in his earlier developmental years, and in the first year especially, the likelihood is that he will survive this normative crisis and emerge a maturer person. Where, however, too many emotional gaps have been left, as a result of previous adverse experiences, the period of adolescence may give rise to more intense difficulties. Depending on how this period is handled, there is still a good chance of the crisis being used as an opportunity even to put right earlier adversities and so help the individual to emerge a more complete personality.

Adoptees in general seemed to link their strong differences and disagreements with their parents with the fact of their adoption. Their adoption provided an easy explanation of why they could not get on with father or mother. The greater the conflict the more the tendency to attribute it to the fact of adoption. This is how most of them came to feel at this stage an intense need to know more about their original parents, their genealogy and about themselves.

Where the relationship with the adoptive family was a reasonably good one, the developmental task at this stage appeared to be a final effort to integrate the two sets of parents within the adolescent's identity. There seems to be no obvious reason why, under favourable

102

conditions, an adoptee cannot develop a firm identity on the concept of two sets of parents. Many immigrants' children, as already stated, successfully integrate aspects from their new culture with those from their parents' original one. In fact, attempting to cut oneself off from one's cultural origins is usually a characteristic of alienated personalities. Most adoptees in the sample, except those who felt too estranged from their parents, saw their adoptive parents as forming their primary frame of reference, and their natural origins as contributing a minor but important part towards the formation of their identity.

It was stated earlier that a great number of adoptees found it difficult to align themselves with more than the first generation of their parents' genealogy, implying that the adoption situation does not usually make this easy or possible. The suggestion was that their descent had to be based on the birth-parents' background. Mr Tait's comments were illustrative of the feelings of others:

I knew I was adopted since I was five or six but as far as I remember the subject was talked about only once or twice since . . . My parents were kind people but very isolated. We had few relatives calling and we had no habit of calling on others. My parents' relatives meant nothing to me and I must have meant nothing to them . . . When I was fifteen or sixteen I was very curious to know 'who I was' and especially to know about my natural parents and their families. With your adoptive family you can only go as far back as they are and not beyond. But with your natural ones you feel you want to go further back . . .

Similar comments were made by other adoptees who did not feel they had been helped to develop deep enough genealogical roots.

The adoptees, who at the time of the search were under twenty, were the only ones whose search seemed to be a continuation of their adolescent experiences. At least two others, who were in their early twenties, were going through a state of delayed adolescence at this point trying to establish their individuality and difference from their parents. All were going through a great upheaval at the time with a considerable amount of acting-out behaviour directed mostly towards the parents or parental surrogate figures. These adoptees had a common characteristic in that they all perceived their adoptive home relationships as 'unhappy' or 'deceptive' or their parents impossible to live with, the latter hardly being an uncommon comment from adolescents who are not adopted. Three of them had lost both their parents before or during adolescence and their feelings of loss were mixed with considerable anger and distress. The rest were still at odds with their adoptive parents or were so troubled within themselves that they viewed the search either as a way of hitting back at the parents or as something that would bring relief.

Miss Smith was eagerly wanting to be seventeen to be able to enquire about her origins at Register House. She had known about her adoption since she was a child but she was going through a very difficult period, feeling very hostile towards her parents and trying to be different from them in every possible way. She attributed the difficulties to disagreements between her parents and to her intensified wish to find her birth-mother being unsympathetically received by her parents:

> I've just got to find out because my adopted parents and I
> haven't got anything in common and people say it could be
> because of my original background. This has been affecting me
> in the last two years and it makes me feel sort of funny with
> everyone. In my parents' home everything has to be spotless.
> You were always getting told off for putting something down in
> the wrong place. They don't like my friends, they think they are
> rough because some ride motor-bikes . . . Well, my parents
> and I just don't see eye to eye. Up until five months ago I
> couldn't stay out after half-past ten . . . They just didn't agree
> with the people I was mixing with and I think friends count a
> lot . . . I tried to meet my parents half-way but they still refused
> to have my friends in the house . . . I get on better with them
> now that I am away . . . they told me that if I refuse to go back
> to the family they are going to unadopt me. I don't know how
> they are going to do it, but they want to. And they want to
> adopt someone else. I can see their point of view. They still
> want to be a family . . . I don't think they will adopt any more
> girls though. Mind you, if anyone criticised my parents I could
> put up a fight for them . . .

Miss Smith's relationship with her parents had other elements which pointed to a very strained situation with a lot of parental splitting and acting-out behaviour. The normative crisis of adolescence assumed greater proportions in this case and the adoptee was using her adoption and her original genealogy in her attempt to demonstrate that she was a different and separate person. Her desire to pursue her enquiries when she reached the permitted age of seventeen seemed indicative of the degree of her conflict with her family.

Miss Reid's was another similar case. She had become estranged from her parents because they 'disagree on everything'. She identified with 'minority' groups because she saw herself as a member of a minority group, i.e., adopted. She was critical of her parents for being prejudiced towards coloured and young people in general and remarked that her mother's 'unkind remarks' about minority groups must refer to herself, too. She had known about her adoption since the age of four, but it was only around the age of sixteen that she started to feel curious about her real parents:

> It is like as somebody says something, talks about something and I want to know more about it so that I can understand . . . It is unnatural not to. If you know half the fact about your adoption you will try to know the other half . . . My parents must know how they came to adopt me but I don't want to ask them. I would rather find out for myself. As we do not talk to each other now the only way is to find out myself . . .

When communication between the adolescent adoptee and the parent did not exist or when the parent was dead, then the adoptee was searching beyond his adoptive family for confirmatory experiences about himself. The adoptive parent was not necessarily rejected as an identification figure except where the relationship was experienced as very negative and destructive. Otherwise the adopted adolescents seemed to continue to model themselves on the only parents they knew, but they could not obliterate the reality of the other set of parents, part of whom they wished to integrate in themselves.

The crisis of middle age

For a small group of adoptees the search did not start till they were in their forties or fifties. Though they had thought about it before, they suddenly felt a great need, mostly to meet their original mothers. They saw this as a last opportunity to do something for their original mother who would now be elderly and perhaps in need of some kind of support. A man of fifty felt that he had to find his mother now as 'time was running out':

> As I am getting older the urge is greater. It crossed my mind before but there was not the same urgency as now. My birth-mother must be nearing seventy now. She will be old enough to wonder and may be quite pleased to see me . . . another few years and she may not be there . . . I may be able to help her or she may help me. At the present time I have no blood relationships at all in the world. My wife and my adopted son are not blood relationships. I may regret it in ten years time for not trying to find out earlier.

Another adoptee, now in her mid-forties, was on anti-depressants and her doctor suggested that she was depressed because of her middle age. During this period her wish to meet her original mother became an 'obsessional' preoccupation. She wanted to meet her to find out what she looked like and whether there were any blood relatives alive:

> I want to know if she is happy . . . as I am . . . we will become or hope to become close friends, my mother and I . . . I had a very close relationship with my adoptive mother and I have missed her since she died three years ago. I would not have tried to find her if my adoptive parents were alive, but this may be the last chance . . .

Mr Thin, now in his late forties, was divorced from his wife and had no contact with his children. He felt very lonely and had taken to drink:

> I am feeling futile and lonely; I have no brothers and no sisters, having been brought up by two old ladies. My natural mother could be of help to me and I could be of help to her. She may need me as I suddenly feel I need her. We could do something for each other.

The emotional needs of the adoptees in this age group manifested themselves through generalised depression and low feelings. They tended to project their own needs as possibly being those of the unknown parent. Hence the urgency to meet them and help them. Like adolescence, the crisis of middle age seems to stir or bring to the surface earlier unintegrated parts of oneself. Whilst most people are able to cope with this new phase of life and survive its depressive side, for some the task is too great and external help may be necessary. Adoptees in this group were still hoping to get support and nourishment from their original parents in order to survive this phase. They seemed to find it hard to give them up even at this late stage.

Inner pressures predominating

In the examples given earlier, a particular external or normative crisis appeared to increase personal stress and generate an intense desire to search into one's origins. However, in some cases the crisis consisted of the intolerable level reached by unexplainable internal strain. The latter required only a minor outside pressure to become impossible to manage or control. The mother of three young children had been thinking of searching into her background for some time, but she put if off until recently when she felt she 'had to establish her true identity'. She was feeling increasingly desolate and depressed and she felt that she could not put off the search any longer. She hoped that the search would help her with what she called her 'identity problems':

> I felt I had to find out about my true identity . . . to find out exactly who I was and what my original name had been. I would like to know about my father as I have been told so many bad things about my mother . . . Identity means a great deal to me and I started feeling in this way especially since I became a parent. Recently I have been feeling more depressed and despondent . . . I am worried how much I have taken after my original mother and how far my children are taking after me and what this is going to do to them.

Strength of the motivation

Although all the adoptees were pursuing certain definite goals, the strength of their motivation and the degree of urgency differed. This seemed to depend on the purpose of the search and on the adoptees' circumstances. As a general rule, the adoptees whose goal was to find their original parents were more strongly motivated than those searching for information (see Appendix: Table 7.1). The adoptees of the first group were more determined and there was a sense of great urgency about their enquiries. No amount of persuasion or explanation could have influenced them towards a different course of action at this late stage. The whole search had built up into a great event with considerable feeling being invested in the process and the expectations of the outcome.

Again the most highly motivated adoptees were those from the first group who had a poor image of themselves and who perceived their family relationships as mainly unsatisfactory (Table 7.1). The high degree of their motivation seemed to be equalled only by their high expectations from the search. Those adoptees in this group who failed to find their parents after the initial attempt were still the most highly motivated in their continued efforts. To have given up would have left them with a greater sense of desolation.

In contrast, there was less determination and urgency among those adoptees who described more satisfactory family relationships, who had a more positive self-image and who were feeling less inner pressure. Most of these adoptees featured in the group which was wanting additional information.

Summary

Adolescence was the most common period when adoptees first thought of enquiring into their origins and genealogy. The strength of this desire usually reflected the type of family relationships prevailing at home. The more unsatisfactory these relationships were the greater the adolescent's desire to search into his background. Even when such feelings were strong, however, only a very small number of adoptees acted on them and the eventual decision to search was motivated by some crisis in the adoptee's subsequent life situation. Past experience combined with current life situations tended to start off the search for the parent or for background information. Current crises gave rise to feelings of 'abandonment' and 'loss' and generated the search. These crises seemed to trigger off the original experience of 'abandonment' by the natural parents.

Hopes and expectations

> Maybe I am looking for something I never had and which
> I may never get, but until I meet her I will never know.
> I am hoping I can have a relationship with her. She is flesh
> and blood and there must be a tie . . . I've got lots of friends
> but I want somebody that is like me, that's part of me.
>
> > Female adoptee

The adoptees set out in their search with expectations that they hoped would be fulfilled. It was hoped, for instance, that the desired meeting with the natural parent(s) or the background information gained would ultimately lead to certain personal and emotional satisfactions. At this particular stage in their lives they maintained that these needs could not be met by other people close to them, such as husband, wife or children, or the adoptive parents. Those who had experienced all these possible sources of satisfaction still felt that something was missing. Consequently high expectations were often placed on the search and its outcome.

Of the forty-two adoptees whose goal was to meet their first parents, twenty-five (or three out of every five) were keen to meet only their mothers. Of the remaining seventeen, two were interested in meeting their fathers and the rest showed interest in both parents. The great preference for the mother was not a characteristic of the female adoptees only but of both sexes. A possible explanation for this preoccupation was that adoptees viewed the mother as the person who 'gave them up' and therefore as the one who could now make it up to them.

In contrast to adoptees in search of their parents, those seeking background information were predominantly interested in particulars relating to both parents.

THE EXPECTATIONS OF ADOPTEES SEARCHING FOR THEIR
ORIGINAL PARENTS

The forty-two adoptees whose goal was to meet their natural parents hoped to satisfy one main need from this encounter: this was to hear from their parents 'why' they were given up for adoption and whether they had been 'wanted' and 'loved'. Many hoped that through exploring and discussing these aspects they would be able to establish a 'friendly', 'close' or 'loving' relationship with the parent(s) or with other blood relatives. Adoptees in general wanted to see their original parents as loving and caring, but the fact of their surrender was preventing them from completing this picture. They were hoping to hear from their parents that they had been 'wanted' and 'loved' and that it had been circumstances beyond their control which had made the surrender necessary. The confirmation of a 'good' and 'caring' parental figure would help to raise their own self-esteem as 'caring' and 'good' people.

The need to know the 'why' of their adoption and whether they were 'wanted' appeared to be of great importance to the adoptees' self-image and identity and to the valuation of themselves. Answers to such questions and explanations appeared necessary to help them understand themselves and their adoption situation. As long as such questions remained unanswered they tried to speculate or create fantasies. Active fantasies of rejection, of being unwanted or of being a foundling, or of being nobody's child, were indicative of their poor self-image. Such fantasies reinforced the feelings of rejection and the general unhappiness surrounding them. Speculations and suppositions of this kind implied, also, anger towards the original parents for deserting them, but in the wake of their present 'unhappiness' and high expectations this could not be openly expressed. The angry feelings of two adoptees towards their birth-mothers were voiced only after they had met them, the encounter ending in the rejection now of the parents by the adoptees.

There was no doubt that many adoptees, including even some of those who were searching for background information only, perceived their surrender as a form of rejection and abandonment by their original parents and they said so. Those feeling more disillusioned felt greatly rejected and they were very critical of their mothers for surrendering them. Those who were told or found that their mothers had loved and wanted them, but that a combination of circum-stances had made it difficult for the mothers to care for them, were more understanding and less bitter. Some of the latter wondered, however, how it was possible 'for a parent that loved you to put you up for adoption'. The poor image that many adoptees had of them-selves was perhaps reinforced by feelings of having been given up because they were unwanted or bad.

110

One adoptee, with a very low opinion of himself and an unsatisfactory adoptive home, felt very 'rejected' by his original mother and was extremely critical of her for putting him up for adoption. He was not prepared to show any understanding for her possible circumstances at the time. Feelings about the poor relationship with his adoptive mother seemed to be transferred to the natural mother. He saw the latter as being solely responsible for his surrender:

> It is my mother who put me up for adoption; it is she who rejected me. She should not have given me away. I cannot understand how a mother can do this sort of thing. I must meet her and find out from her why she did this to me.

Another adoptee who was also not prepared to make allowances for his natural mother was more bitter because he had heard that she kept an older illegitimate child:

> I would like to know why it was me she had to put up for adoption. I couldn't give up my two kids. Why a person should put a child up for adoption is beyond me. I recently found out that there was no stress or financial difficulties, so why give me up? It is difficult to stop blaming her for what she has done to me.

Mr Simpson felt like this not because his adoption was unsatisfactory—he saw it as fairly satisfactory—but because he couldn't be at 'peace' with himself until he found the reasons behind his surrender. Another adoptee who saw her adoption as a failure and whose parents implied that her original mother was not 'a nice person to know', was finding it difficult 'to understand who she was' without knowing the circumstances of her mother and those of her adoption. She pictured her original mother 'as a street-walker and a slut who did it for money'. Yet she could not identify with her adoptive parents and thought that her mother must have been 'good and warm hearted' because she herself was like that and this quality in her could only have come from her natural mother. She was anxious to meet her mother and ask her why she put her up for adoption and whether she was a wanted child:

> If ever I had a baby out of wedlock I wouldn't have it adopted. My children mean a tremendous lot to me. Either my mother or my father must have had such feelings for me . . . then why

111

give me up? Was there something wrong with me or with them? I have this obsession about being adopted and my mother is the only one who can help me to understand.

One adoptee who described her adoption as unhappy wanted to meet her mother to ask her both the reasons for putting her up for adoption and whether she knew at the time what kind of home she was being adopted into: 'I can't believe she would have let me go if she knew . . . not if she loved me; it is terrible if she did know and yet she let me go.'

The small number of adoptees who came to know that their original mothers had abandoned them in a Home, and disappeared, felt terribly hurt. They wanted to find their mothers and confront them with their situation. They still wanted to hear from them whether they had been 'loved' as they could not tolerate the possibility that they might not have been wanted: 'It is too much to carry— you can't believe it that your own flesh and blood did this to you.' A young woman, who was expecting her first child at the time of the search, had been told that her original mother had deserted her in a foster home when she was a few weeks old. Now she badly wanted to meet her mother to find out what sort of person she was:

> What is there worse than being told that your mother did not want you? You feel unhappy and bitter; how can you feel different? If she cared she would have made an effort to find me. She knew where I was adopted. So I must have not been wanted. It makes me shudder when I think of it. If she kept me even under hardship I would have appreciated it for what she had tried to do. And yet I want to find her and learn from her why she did this to me and see for myself what kind of person she is.

Mrs Claridge, who had a scar on her back, was convinced that this was caused by her natural mother and that the authorities removed her because of this. She never asked her adoptive parents about it but with the death of the latter she was seized with the urge to find her original mother and establish for herself what kind of person she was and whether they could become friends. Some adoptees were afraid that they might do to their children what their parents did to them. In the same way that some attributed their good qualities to their natural parents, denying the adoptive parents' contribution, others were afraid that their parents' 'bad' qualities might have been transmitted. As they believed strongly that 'good' and 'bad' is a matter of heredity, their fears were real to them and made them anxious and apprehensive. If they could establish that their original parents were 'good' people, this would enhance their faith in themselves and especially their own 'goodness'.

A number of adoptees wanted to know from their mothers whether they 'regretted' giving them up and two of them described what they thought was their original mothers coming to collect them but being stopped by the adoptive parents. As these were memories going back to the ages of seven and nine it was difficult not to conclude that they were fantasied material. These two adoptees pieced together their thoughts retrospectively as they only found out about their adoption in their mid-teens.

I must have been seven or eight at the time and I remember this woman coming to our house. She looked like me and she asked me, 'Are your parents dead? I must tell you I am your mother.' Afterwards I heard my adoptive mother say to her, 'I told you not to come here'. Of course at the time I didn't know I was adopted. It was some years later before I found out.

Even if such accounts are to be accepted as fantasies, they imply that some adoptees wished that their natural mothers had claimed them. However, as similar thoughts were described by adoptees who didn't know at the time that they were adopted, it must be that the entertained fantasy is not unique to adopted children but also to non-adopted ones who possibly find their home life at the time unsatisfactory. An escape mechanism is to fantasy another set of exclusively good parents. Whereas most adopted and non-adopted children will eventually accept their home life and its natural limitations, in the case of adopted children who view their relationships as too unsatisfactory the expectation of an idealised set of parents is continued not as a fantasy but as a real possibility.

Mrs Drummond was certain that her mother had 'regrets' for giving her up and hoped that meeting her would help her to understand why she had to do it:

She must be thinking of me and wondering what happened to me. I must find her and let her tell me why I was given up. I am myself a very warm and spontaneous person and she must be like me. Since my father died I have been feeling the

need for a friendship and someone to be very close to. People
say that what you've never had you never miss; well in my case
I don't think that is true . . . it's hard to say what I am looking
for—it is something you know within yourself but you can't
say it . . . but I think we could both gain out of this if she's
willing. I'm looking for something for myself but it can bring
her happiness also. She must have regrets . . . I know I couldn't
have a child and not think. She can have regrets but perhaps
it can be so painful sometimes to be reminded of it. But I feel if I
don't do it now I'll never do it and it'll live with me all my life.

Miss Vaughan, who was estranged from her adoptive parents,
disliked the idea that she might have taken after them in character.
She was convinced that her original mother was loving and accepting
and that she took these qualities from her. She wanted to believe
that her mother surrendered her only because of her special circumstances but that now they might do a lot for each other.

The need to know 'why' they were put up for adoption featured
in almost all the adoptees' comments but obviously this was of
greater significance to some than to others: 'I would naturally
want to know why she fostered me out . . .' or 'why she put me into
a home'; 'how she managed before parting with me', 'why, why,
why . . . and why did she never make contact . . . maybe she thinks
I have got a good enough life and she does not want to interfere . . .
but I want to hear the circumstances from her.'

There was also the hope, expressed by many, of meeting the natural
mother and establishing a close friendly relationship with her.
They talked of being able then to do things for each other. They said
how they 'missed out' in previous relationships and hoped that the
natural mothers would provide the 'love and warmth they never had'.
They spoke with real feeling about their misery and desolation and
about their urgent need for a parent 'to care' for them. In less sad
cases it was a hope 'for a friendship' because of loneliness or 'the
void within me':

I feel isolated and empty. I am like an island and I feel I have
nobody. If I meet my mother I may get close to her—something
I was never able to do with my adoptive mother. I may be in
for a shattering surprise if I find her, but I cannot stop now.
I have nobody to turn to . . . My husband and children are
not the same . . .

Mrs Braid, a young married woman with two children, was feeling 'desolate and abandoned' and did not feel that she 'belonged to anyone'. Her marriage was going through a very difficult stage at the time and she entertained high hopes from a possible meeting with her mother: 'I want to be mothered by her and to have her around if possible. Someone to lay my head on her shoulders and cry . . . I realise I may be unrealistic but this is how I feel.'

Mrs Braid succeeded in tracing a half-brother who tried to explain to her that 'their' mother was not interested in meeting her. She could not believe it and persisted in wanting to see her and hear from her herself that she did not wish any contact. Not only was her birth mother her last hope for support, but to accept her as uncaring was raising real anxieties about her own attitude towards her two young children whom she deserted once.

The need to find somebody to 'belong to' was mostly felt by those who had lost both parents or those who were feeling very unhappy, 'desolate and empty'. There was a general fantasy that the original mother had somewhere established a 'nice' home life within which the adoptees would find what had been missing from their lives. The fantasied parent was not only more giving and more warm but less demanding than the adoptive one.

Mrs Forfar, married and with two young children, felt 'rejected' by her adoptive parents and by an older sister. She had wanted to trace her mother since the age of seventeen or eighteen but had chosen not to because she was afraid she might not be able to cope with her feelings if she were disappointed. Now she feels she can cope with it. Meeting her first mother should help her not only to understand what it was she missed in her previous relationships but also to have someone she could really call her own:

There must be someone somewhere interested in me and my children. I never felt I belonged in my parents' family and recently we were estranged. My mother sends cards and presents to all her other grandchildren but not to mine . . . If my original mother and myself meet and it does not work out at least I will know. I will not be heartbroken. I will still have my family. On the other hand we may be able to become friends and my children will have a grandmother.

The real existence of a parental figure, who was often fantasied as warm-hearted and caring, apparently made it difficult for adoptees who felt unhappy to relinquish the fantasy until they tested it: 'I am not interested to find out my father because my adoptive father was nicer to me than my adoptive mother . . . It is a mother I want to establish a close relationship with and to have someone to turn to. Unless I meet her I will not know.' Another adoptee who was feeling disillusioned and lonesome was looking for someone 'to want me and to care for me . . . If she does not want me when face to face with her then that is that. I need someone who will want me . . . make me feel secure . . . someone who loves me . . . I never got this feeling from anyone.'

Some other adoptees were in two minds about meeting their original mother and whilst hoping that such a meeting would be helpful, they were also apprehensive of initiating contact that they might not wish to continue. A young student who was hoping to find her natural mother and become close friends was also apprehensive of the consequences in case it did not work out as she wanted: 'She may want to continue to see me and I may not. What do I do then?' Another said: 'She may have needs which I may be expected to meet'. A similar fear was expressed by a third, who remarked: 'How do you then get rid of her?'

The accounts of many adoptees in this group illustrated the difficulty of coming to terms with the loss of someone who has not been experienced as real. Such acceptance appears to be made easier by the revelation of the adoptive status and the sharing of detailed meaningful information which makes the natural parents sound real and individual. Failing this, the adoptee's over-idealisation of the original parent can make it difficult for him to come to reasonable terms with painful reality. There is some similarity here with the person who loses a limb; an over-idealisation of normality and physical health makes it hard for him to accept the partial loss. Miss Smith, who was going through a difficult adolescent stage, had no wish to develop a relationship with her first mother but wanted to meet her in person to find out a number of things from her. Only a physical meeting would be meaningful to her, 'otherwise I cannot understand through other people talking about her'. For her, only the natural mother in person could make the experience feel real:

Well I would like to meet her and find out for myself what she actually is like. Find out what sort of person she is and of course her background. I was about eighteen months old when

I was adopted. I want to find out what happened before. I would like to meet her but I don't want to upset her. I don't want to hurt anyone but I don't think anyone would ever get over losing a child, no matter how she loses it. If I find out that it is sort of going to hurt her, if she is married and got other children, she might not want to remember, so I won't bring that up . . . But if I had a child and I was unmarried, I still wouldn't have it adopted. If I meet her I could never call her 'mother'. My actual hopes are to find her and to see what she looks like and to find out what background my original parents have got and generally find out why I was adopted. The reason why. Then, if I can talk with her about it to put it more clear in my mind. I think that would help me a bit to become more clear. I would also like to know whether I have any brothers and sisters and what sort of life I might have lived if I hadn't been adopted.

Some female adoptees who lost their fathers with whom they had close relationships and who were disappointed by their mothers' re-marriage, were now searching for their original fathers as a replacement of the adoptive one. Mrs McClure said:

I was always close to my father, we had so much in common. I missed him greatly when he died. I was then only fifteen and I grieved for him . . . I have never found myself again. I feel empty and depressed. My main hope now is to find my natural father and see if there is a chance of us getting to know each other. My adoptive father was Cornish and I learned that my natural father was Cornish, too. If so he must be warm and kind like my adoptive father was . . .

It was important to most adoptees to know whether the original parent was alive or dead. The few who established that the sought-after parent was dead, seemed generally to accept the fact and to say that at least they knew where they stood: 'There is nothing more to do.' But two of them couldn't believe it and continued to search in spite of evidence pointing to the certainty of death. Both of them appeared under considerable stress. It is possible that by accepting the fact of death and giving up the search they would then have to face their unhappiness and loneliness. As long as there was some hope that the parent was alive, and until the adoptee met him or her, it seemed difficult for some to come to terms with the loss, which had happened many years earlier:

> Well I think I would like to find if she is still alive and what she is doing. I was told that she is dead but no one could tell me where she was buried. I don't believe it or perhaps I don't want to. I am not clear what I am after. I don't think I know within myself; just the satisfaction of knowing what she is and what she is like . . . I've got a family of my own, I've got two kids of my own, we are starting a life of our own, but there is still a loose end and I just want to tie it up. It's like a string with an end hanging out you don't know where to put it. Meeting my mother may help me to do just that . . . it's a thing you have got to do.

Two other adoptees who learned that their original mothers were dead felt greatly helped by visiting the graves and 'seeing' for themselves. The reality of the graves seemed to help them to start looking at their loss in a different way.

THE EXPECTATIONS OF ADOPTEES SEARCHING FOR BACKGROUND INFORMATION

Adoptees in the previous group were mostly interested to meet their parents to learn from them 'why' they were given up for adoption and whether they were wanted. Most of them were also hoping to establish a relationship with their original mother, father, or both. Adoptees in the Background Information group were hoping that the information obtained would help to 'supplement' or 'complete' their knowledge of themselves.

The main wish of those in this group was to obtain additional information about their sociological and biological backgrounds because they felt they did not know enough. This was either because of reticence on the part of the parents, or inhibition about asking on the part of the adoptees, or exceptionally because the parents did not know enough themselves.

Though the idea of meeting their natural parents held some attraction for some of these adoptees, they generally maintained that this was not what they were interested in: 'There is no point in meeting my natural parents; we would be like two strangers meeting.' Another adoptee remarked: 'I do not particularly want to form a

118

relationship with my mother. If we met it would be like two strangers being introduced to each other. There is no guarantee that we would like each other. After all we do not like all strangers we are introduced to.'

Mrs Swan connected her uncertainties about herself with her lack of knowledge about her origins and remarked:

You do wonder who you belong to and where you come from and it isn't until you realise that you don't know that you begin to wonder. Most other people take so much for granted that they just never have to query it—it isn't until you find out that you don't know what you are or where you are from, what kind of people you come from . . . No, I don't think I would like to meet my original mother. She may be married with her own family and I just don't think it is fair to her—everyone is entitled to make a mistake or two. I don't have any bitter feelings against her for having given me away or rejected me. I would have liked to know who my father was and the circumstances that resulted in my birth . . . When you have children of your own, if you are adopted, and they don't bear any strict resemblance to anyone, you wonder who they took after . . .

A young woman, who recently lost her adoptive mother with whom she had a good relationship, did not want to get in contact with her natural parents, but only wanted

to find out a bit more without having to embarrass them. They have got their own lives and they probably wouldn't want to meet me. One would certainly, however, like to know more about them—what they did and what their backgrounds are . . . I have never harboured any resentment against them. If I saw my mother and she didn't measure up to my expectations, it would be rather a blow. It is best not to.

Mr Edwards, who for a year now had been having migraine attacks and was feeling very restless, hoped that finding out about his background might help him to be more relaxed: 'Knowing who my parents were, whether I have any brothers and sisters, and who I look like may help me to be less worried about things. But I never dreamt of going to find my birth-mother.' Other adoptees hoped that knowledge about their genealogy and origins would be of help to them personally: 'If I can attach some real names to myself and come to know some tangible things it may help me to feel less lonesome.'

Again what adoptees were trying to say was how difficult it was to accept their situation without having something real or concrete about their past. One young married man said:

> Even a photo might help; everybody remarks on how similar you are to your father but in fact it is the mannerisms and not any physical characteristic they refer to. I often ask myself; who do I look like? If I had some description of my original parents it might help me to recognise myself.

The adoptees who could not see much point in a meeting between themselves and their natural parents found that knowledge about their origins and 'cultural' past of their forebears was necessary for a full understanding of themselves, but that there was no need for a meeting. One of them remarked: 'It could be embarrassing to them and to me. What's the point anyway? If you have never met them before it is like two strangers meeting. But I would like to know more about them as people and through them to understand myself better.' A female social worker who claimed to have had a satisfactory home life was hoping that through the search she would come to know more about her adoption and about her origins because she found her parents evasive:

> I don't really want to meet my birth-mother as I don't feel a great deal towards her to want to meet her because I have never known her . . . but when I realise I don't know who I belong to and where I come from and what kind of people my original parents were, then I am curious to learn more about them . . . I was adopted so young I've never known any other parents so I cannot be expected to have any yearnings for them . . . it would be terribly complicated anyway . . . But I feel there is a part of me I don't know about and until I find out I won't be satisfied. It could help me to understand myself better and through it others.

'Since I never knew my mother', said Mr Newsom, 'I don't think there would be any type of meaningful dialogue between us . . . but I would like to have known about her and her situation when I was a young boy.' A similar comment was made by another adoptee who said: 'I am not really interested in my first mother as a person. The truth is she means nothing to me especially as I had a fairly contented life. But I am curious to know a bit more about myself and my background.'

One adoptee who claimed to have had a happy home life was curious to see if Register House held any information in addition to that which his parents had already shared with him:

I never felt the lack of a blood-tie and never felt that my parents were only my adoptive parents. But my parents knew very little about my original ones and I wanted to find out such things as the part of the country I come from and where I was born. Everybody likes to know about these things; they are part of you and when you don't know it is like something important missing.

The parents of Miss Gibbs shared with her a fair amount of information about the circumstances of her adoption. She started on her search hoping to find some information about the place where she was born and the part of the country in which her original parents happened to live:

I would never seek out my natural mother or go and stay with her . . . For one thing I wouldn't like to hurt or let down the people who gave me so much when I most needed it. To me my original mother is an outsider and she means nothing to me. I don't think anybody can take the place of the people who brought you up. I frankly don't see any point in pursuing this any more.

Fears of incest

Only four adoptees connected the desire to identify their natural parents with incestuous fears. The fear was about unknowingly committing incest with a natural sibling. Freud[1] in 1900 drew attention to incestuous tendencies being present in all children. If so, adopted children must have reality based anxieties and it could explain their deep need to know about their origins and their first families. Yet only a very small number of those covered by the study expressed such fears. A young adoptee in his early twenties indirectly attributed some of his sexual inhibitions to incestuous fears:

121

You meet a girl and you ask her out and suddenly you think: this could be my sister; how do I know.? Your first thought is not to turn up but the idea keeps coming back . . . after all you don't know do you? It could happen . . . the first thing I would like to ask my natural mother is whether I had any sisters or brothers . . .

Another adoptee said that when she got to know a boy-friend well she used to question him closely about his parents and the place he was born. She hoped that this would give her some clue about a possible link. When eventually she met her husband, however, she wrote to Register House for information only after their marriage: 'I got terribly anxious whilst waiting for a reply to come. My husband thought I was making a lot of fuss but I wanted to make sure . . . I didn't write before I married because it didn't bother me in the same way.'

Considering the very small number of adoptees who each year try to find their original parents, in the whole group, anxieties about incest should not be exaggerated. After all, those who never make enquiries are unlikely to know more about any possible family of their natural parents which has been created after the adoption. If such tendencies, conscious or unconscious do exist, the vast majority of adoptees must be dealing with them in ways other than through searching for their birth parents. It again appears that other factors or difficulties need to be present before a condition becomes intolerable, and the adoptee sets out in search of his origins. Because of the possibility of incest, however, it is important that adoption agencies place children over a wide area, avoiding the recruitment of adoptive parents from the same locality in which the natural parents also live.

Summary

In general, the adoptees' expectations from the search were closely related to their feelings about their past relationships, about themselves and the nature of the current stress. Though all adoptees wanted to know why they were given up and whether previously they had been wanted and loved by their original parents, this need varied in degree. The more disillusioned and unhappy they felt the greater the need to have their answers directly from the original parents. Most of these were also hoping to develop a close caring relationship with their first parents. This group included many of those who had lost one or both adoptive parents or who felt very disappointed and angry about the outcome of their adoption. The more satisfied the adoptees felt with their adoptive families and with themselves, the greater the possibility that they were now expecting to obtain, through the search, information that would help to complete their selves. Almost all the adoptees implied how difficult it was for them to accept the loss of their original parents without coming to see them as real people through some meaningful descriptions or possibly through physical contact.

What I wanted from my original mother was affection, which
I never had . . . I pictured her as a loving woman and I have
been disappointed. After the first couple of meetings with her
I was not interested in her any more. She wanted to continue
the relationship but I didn't.

Young male adoptee

The majority of adoptees were uncertain and vague about the type of
information they were likely to obtain from the records at Register
House. This was possibly due to the fact that few of them had
previously seen a full certificate which was an extract from the
register of births. All were hoping that they would be given substantial
information about their natural parents and their original genealogical background. Those who were keen to meet their natural parents
were also hopeful that Register House might be able to provide
particulars about the present whereabouts of their parents.

Though many adoptees were hoping to obtain particulars that
would ultimately lead to the finding of the original parent, the
actual provision of the mother's address at the time of surrender
came as a pleasant surprise. It fired their imagination further and
acted as a strong impetus to continue the search. Adoptees were
asked how far they would have been satisfied if no address had
been provided and whether they would have stopped their search at
that point. Those who were strongly motivated to meet their parents,
and who felt most pressurised from within, maintained that they
would have carried on irrespective of what information they were
given. Mrs McDonald's comment was representative of that of
others in this group: 'Even if there was no address provided, I
would still continue to find out. It is not just curiosity; it is a feeling
you get because of something within you which needs satisfaction;
when you get this feeling you want to find out. Nothing can stop
you.'

A few adoptees who were less strongly motivated for the search
implied that they might have stopped there but that the address

either increased their curiosity or made them feel obliged to continue once they had gone so far. Two of those who set out originally to obtain only background information now felt the urge to try and trace their natural parents:

> Before you set out you tell yourself that this is the last effort and that after it you will accept what you are and leave it at that. But once you get an address with a name and a number you feel you cannot stop; the address keeps you going; perhaps if it was not the address it would have been something else.

Reaction to information gained

Eight out of ten adoptees were glad of what information they obtained. This included most of those who for the first time found what they described as 'unpalatable' facts about themselves. However, all of them were disappointed at the paucity of the information available. With few exceptions, the information was not up to their expectations and they were critical of the system for depriving them of what some described as their 'birthright to know.' Though most of them obtained certain tangible information with which they were not previously acquainted, they still found it unsatisfactory and there was a general wish for more 'meaningful' information. 'All I got', remarked one of them, 'was a name and address and this cannot be the whole of me'; 'I was glad for what I got,' said another, 'but it does not feel enough; it doesn't take you very far.' For a minority the information was a confirmation of what they already knew and there was nothing new to add. There was equal dissatisfaction about the nature of the particulars both from those searching for their original parents and the ones looking for background information.

The aspect of illegitimacy

A large proportion of children adopted are illegitimate and many of those in the sample were aware of this and recognised that it was unlikely they would have been adopted if they were legitimate. This did not stop them, however, from having certain feelings about illegitimacy and the assumed stigma it carries. For some the revelation

125

of their illegitimacy came when they enquired at Register House and this was felt to be distressing. They maintained that this possibility had not entered their minds before, or if it had, they were still hoping to find that their natural parents were married: 'I like to think that I had parents who were married and that they were killed during the war. It pleased me to think like this.' After finding out about their original illegitimate status they built up fantasies of mothers who were 'promiscuous' or 'street-walkers' and they were now hoping to establish that this was not so. They were hoping to hear that though illegitimate they were the result of a 'love-affair' that could not end in marriage because of parental hostility or because of the war or of other similar circumstances:

> I always thought I had been adopted because something had happened to my parents. I never even thought of my father as not being my mother's husband. This came as a shock to me; I mean, I am illegitimate and we all know what people think about illegitimacy . . . No, I don't think that adoption wipes out your illegitimacy. I am now holding on to the hope that my mother was not a street-walker.

Confirmation of illegitimate status seemed to play into some adoptees' already negative self-image and gave expression to feelings of shame and inferiority:

> Even if you suspect it that you are illegitimate, it is shattering to find out. You are suddenly left bare and you think, 'I am only a bastard'; you can explain to your children that you are adopted but how do you explain that you are also illegitimate?

A young married man who saw his adoptive status as something which confers 'inferior' status, reacted in a similar way when he found out about his illegitimacy: 'It is very distressing to know that you are a bastard. You don't want anyone to know about it. It is very shameful.' Another couldn't bear to hear the word illegitimacy mentioned in newspapers or on television and thought that everybody who knew her must have been thinking of her being a 'bastard'. Whatever the community thinks about adoption and illegitimacy, more important is the adoptee's own perception of community attitudes and of himself. Perhaps the adoptees in the sample saw society's attitude

126

towards them as being harsher than it really is, perhaps some of this distress was transferred from other unhappy situations and focused onto their illegitimate status: 'My main distress', said Mr Erickson, 'is being a bastard; I am not big enough to tell anybody that I am adopted because they will realise that I am also a bastard.' A girl, recently married, was so shocked to discover that she was illegitimate that she was ill for a fortnight, lying in bed and brooding over it with all sorts of speculations about the type of person her mother was. She maintained that it had never occurred to her before that she was illegitimate.

Four adoptees whose original mothers had unusual surnames that indicated a possible foreign origin were further confused as if their identity had received yet another knock, this time with regard to their original cultural background. They wondered about the mother's nationality and they were worried about the possibility of 'coloured' or 'Negroid' features that might appear in their children. Mrs Crammond was quite upset when she first found that she was illegitimate, and so was her husband. She attributed her darkish complexion—hardly noticeable—to her mother's possible foreign origin:

> My dark skin makes me wonder who I take from. Now that I
> saw my mother's surname I am almost certain that I have Negro
> blood in me. Children at school used to call me nigger and it
> felt awful. I feel I must find her and see what she looks like
> and who my father was . . . Not that I dislike coloured people
> but it is more confusing to be adopted, illegitimate and coloured;
> especially as I never thought of myself as other than Scottish.
> It all becomes more complicated . . .

After twenty years of married life, Mr Duncan only recently shared the fact of his adoption with his wife because of his shame about being illegitimate:

> Perhaps nobody now cares much about illegitimacy, but when
> I was born, a bastard was a bastard . . . this is what is haunting
> me. Not that I am adopted but that I am illegitimate. When I
> was born you were marked if anybody knew you were illegitimate
> . . . Now that I've seen my natural mother's surname [Abdullah]
> I wonder if I've got some cannibal blood in me. What is more
> distressing is that I always pictured myself as Scottish, pure

127

Scottish. I'm still Scottish, of course, but somewhere
there must be some mixed blood in me. So I don't want to
pursue things any further in case this nasty finding is
confirmed . . .

Other adoptees were surprised to find that they were illegitimate because their adoptive parents had made them believe that
their original parents were married. It was not only the fact of
illegitimacy that shook them, but also the fact that their adoptive
parents had 'lied' to them. This proved especially hard for those who
said they had a reasonably good relationship with their parents and
who were now greatly disappointed to realise that they had been
'cushioned' in lies. One of them remarked: 'There was no point for
my mother telling me that my natural parents were married. It was
easier to accept my illegitimacy than to accept that my parents were
not honest with me'; and another:

My parents told me that I had a father and a mother who died.
I now find that my mother was not married. There was no point
for them to fabricate such a story and have me romanticise it.
Perhaps it is difficult for them to realise that a child can
gradually accept even the bitter truth than to have his faith
shaken in later life.

The aspect of legitimacy

As with those adoptees who were distressed to find that they were
illegitimate, so those very few who found that their parents were
married were equally hurt. They could not understand how their
parents could have 'given' them up and they seemed to feel it as a
greater form of rejection than did those whose parents were not
married. They wondered about the kind of parents that give their
children up and they thought of possible neglect or desertion. They
showed generally less understanding towards their natural parents'
possible circumstances at the time, compared with the rest of the
adoptees. Though terribly pleased to find that they were not illegitimate they were keen to find their parents to hear from them why they
were given away: 'If I knew they did not want me I would be most
upset', remarked one of them; 'and yet what else could it signify?',
he added.

Occupational background of natural mother

Though some adoptees had no 'illusions' about the possible occupation of their natural mothers or fathers, many others were hoping to find that their original parents were students or professional people. These hopes were mostly cherished by adoptees of professional or semi-professional occupations or by those who married into middle-class homes. These felt the pressure to prove themselves to their in-laws. Some construed bits of information to fit in with an image of a 'nice' or 'well-spoken' or 'attractive' person who was either a 'teacher' or a 'student', or the daughters or sons of 'well-off families who wanted to hush the fact of illegitimacy'. The truth was that the vast majority of the natural mothers were maids, some were shop assistants, two were nurses and two clerical workers. (Nowadays the biggest single group of women who surrender their children is clerical workers, and then almost equal proportions of professional women, skilled manual workers and women in transport and catering, but very few domestic workers. The nature of employment has changed over the last thirty years and so have the surrendering habits of single mothers.)

Certainly many adoptees who were hoping to meet their mothers were also hoping that the latter would conform to one of the accep table images. Even many of those who were not planning to find them, were hoping to hear that their mother's occupational background would be 'one to be proud of'. Some adoptees were extremely hurt by allusions made by husbands, wives or other relatives concerning their background and they wanted to show them that they were 'as good or better' than anybody else. They staked a lot on the search and when they found out that they were illegitimate or learned about the real mother's 'lowly job', they felt 'crushed' and 'defeated'. Such findings from the search seemed to reinforce an already poor self-image rather than create it. The interpretation put on the findings by Mrs Henderson was indicative of that of a few others:

> The real reason why I tried to find out was the hope that my natural mother was somebody, though deep down I was afraid she might be a tramp . . . I was obsessed about it. You see my adoptive family and my in-laws are very snobbish . . . They have been making cryptic allusions to my background and so I wanted to show them . . . When the information came back from Register House and I read that my original mother was

only a brewery worker I became very distressed. It is two months now and I have not yet told my husband. I hate to think that all she was was a brewery worker. Once I had a desire to meet my mother but not now. If she were a teacher, or a doctor or a nurse it would be different, but a brewery worker I cannot forgive her . . . Sometimes I wish I had not been born.

After this initial disappointment, Mrs Henderson started building up the image of her natural father hoping again to find him or find information about him that would uplift her.

Mrs McDiarmid was looking for a 'warm, loving' person and a mother she could be proud of. She was envious of her husband's family who were 'such a happy one' and as she was at odds with her adoptive family, she wanted to prove that her original mother was of a 'good' family, warm and loving. When she found that her natural mother had been a maid she felt shattered and became distressed and angry. She expressed considerable anger towards her birth-mother for being 'only a maid', dashing all her hopes and expectations. After she recovered from her initial disappointment she again started to build her mother up as a 'warm-hearted' person and worth pursuing, 'in spite of her occupation'.

Because the particulars which many adoptees obtained did not come up to their expectations, or because the search for the original parent was proving futile, some felt 'dazed', 'shocked', 'shattered', 'depressed' or 'confused' after the search. This did not mean that they regretted their action. The confusion and often depression that followed appeared to be related partly to the difficulty of integrating this new factual bit of information with existing fantasied material and partly to the realisation that hopes about the resolution of basic difficulties had not come true.

The search for the original parent(s)

Following the enquiry at Register House, where they obtained a name and address, usually of their natural mother, many adoptees made a number of efforts to locate her. They visited the address given in the original birth certificate but it was rare to find that the same house was still standing or that the occupants had not changed several times over the years. (The average time span between the adoptees' birth and the time of their search was approximately twenty-seven years, a long enough period for many changes to take place.) The result of one adoptee's search was typical:

> We looked up the address where she stayed, but it didn't now exist. It must have been the old part of Glasgow that's been demolished. I am still trying to find out from the electoral registers of the city but it is not easy. There are so many similar names. I am going about it very carefully of course as she might be involved or married and have a family of her own again. But I still would like to find her.

Adoptees, though very keen to meet their original parent(s), were generally concerned not to do it in a way that might be hurtful or upsetting. Mrs Forfar wrote to the address obtained at Register House but the letter was returned because the house had been demolished:

> I don't know how to go about it now. I feel like lost. Perhaps a private investigator is the best sort of thing. They can do it quietly. It sounds rather seedy but it seems to be the only way. But I must think about it more. I don't want to do anything that may hurt her—it would be awful. But having gone this far I feel I couldn't leave it.

Mr Erickson, mentioned earlier, was in a great dilemma and in two minds about what to do after he heard from a relative that his natural mother was now married:

> When I first got her address it was at a time I was feeling very resentful for being put up for adoption. I was going to write angrily and tell her what I thought of her. But when I heard she was married and that her husband's health was not good, I thought it was best left alone . . . Writing might cause a lot of damage . . . I would rather leave it for the time being . . .

The motivation of Mrs Drummond to meet her original mother increased considerably when she heard from some source that her mother had not married: 'If she is not married it is different . . . we may be able to do something for each other'. Because of fear of hurting her original mother this adoptee, like many others, was looking for a kind of agency that would act as intermediary to arrange contact, if both sides wanted it: 'I think we should both be given the chance to meet each other . . . She should be given the chance to say "yes" or "no" now, even if she decided over twenty years ago to give me up . . . You don't know that she is not hoping too for this kind of contact.'

Miss Reid, whose search was closely related to her adolescent strivings and to disagreements with her parents, had at the same time some mixed feelings about a possible meeting and remarked: 'I would be very pleased if my natural mother started enquiring about me. But again there should be a person to arrange it and she should not just turn up at the door. I wouldn't turn up at her door and I wouldn't like her to do so either.'

Adoptees would often spend considerable time in public libraries looking up names in telephone directories or in the electoral roll. When these methods failed—as they often did—some would place advertisements in newspapers. None had had any response to these. Mr Marshall's experience was not untypical of that of other adoptees:

> I first went to the address given by Register House but the houses had been pulled down. Then I went to the public library and looked up addresses but it is such a common name and anyway she may be married and have another name now. I looked up the electoral rolls but there were tens of similar names. When I came to a dead end I put an advert in one of the papers but got no reply. Somebody told me she could have been a nurse and I wrote to the Register for Nurses but they could not help . . . I am kind of lost now for which way to go . . . what do you suggest I do?

Other adoptees visited welfare agencies or children's homes in the area to ask if their adoption had been arranged through them or whether they had been left there as foundlings or otherwise. They regretted the fact that there was no way of even knowing which adoption agency had made the arrangements. Adoptees who were trying hard to get in touch with their natural mothers wanted to believe that the latter were also searching for them. They regularly read the newspaper columns where advertisements of this kind appear and lived in hope of one day coming across an appeal that would refer to themselves. The belief that the natural mother was also searching for them was related to their desperate need to hear that they were wanted and that the surrender was not a form of rejection. One of them said:

After I had my baby I began to think somebody in this world is a person called my mother and I must find her. If she is alive she must also be thinking of me now and perhaps searching for me. I know what it feels to have a child and she must have felt like I did.

Contact established

As a result of their enquiries, eleven adoptees were able to trace a natural parent or a close blood relation. Two adoptees met their natural mothers, one his father, one met both parents and seven others met a blood sibling, a grandparent or an aunt. Mr Craig called at Register House on the first day of his honeymoon. He obtained the address where his natural mother used to live twenty-three years earlier and on the same day he and his wife travelled to the area. There they heard from the present occupants of the house that the mother was now married and living elsewhere in the same city. Accompanied by the tenant of the old house, they went to the new address and waited in the car until the 'friend' went into the house, talked with the mother and then came out with her to the waiting car. Mother and son were introduced to each other 'but it was not a question of open arms'. He asked her if she was 'Ann Duncan' and she said 'Yes'. He then added, 'I am Michael Craig from W . . ., you remember twenty-three years ago?' The mother is reputed to have said 'I expected this for some years; I am glad it happened': 'There was a moment', the adoptee remarked, 'when I suddenly thought I might have the wrong woman.' They talked to each other for some time and then he and his wife were invited into the house where they met the husband and the mother's two children. A further contact followed between them and then the adoptee became weary of his birth-mother's efforts to continue seeing him. He became irritated with her and wanted to bring the contacts to an end because she was not the affectionate woman he pictured.

The criticisms he now expressed about his original mother, including her lack of warmth, were similar to those he voiced about his deceased adoptive mother. There was an obvious transfer of strong negative feeling from the adoptive to the natural mother. It appeared that he was now rejecting his natural mother and doing to her what she did to him when she surrendered him. Asked whether it helped him meeting his first mother he remarked: 'It has helped me considerably. Before there would be my two mothers and I did not know where to turn; I also had expectations that it is obvious she couldn't meet but now I know where I stand. I have no regrets about meeting her.'

Mr Evans, a young labourer with a psychiatric history, was able to locate his natural father by following up the address given on the birth certificate. His parents were in fact married at the time of his birth but he went into the care of the local authority for a short period and was then adopted. In the meantime his original parents divorced and they now had new families. The adoptee went to the little town where his natural parents lived twenty years earlier and enquired at the supplied address. There he was told that his father was now living at another address in the same town. He called at the new address and asked the woman who answered the door whether he could see Mr Jenkins. She told him that he could find Mr Jenkins at the pub round the corner, and the adoptee then left. It turned out later that the woman was his natural father's wife. At the pub he had Mr Jenkins pointed out to him, went up to him, drew him aside and showed him his original birth certificate. He went on:

> After he read the birth certificate he shook hands with me and as we couldn't speak there we went to a room by ourselves. I never said anything much except that I was interested to meet him. There was nothing much to say really. He was pleased to see me and he started to cry. He asked me to forgive him for leaving my mother but he said he had tried his best . . . things had not worked out. He then told me that the same thing was happening with his second wife . . . I felt happier since I met my real father . . . you are closer to your own people. I never felt close to anybody before. I now go and visit his family almost every night but he has eight children and there is no room for me to stay.

A short time after reporting this apparently satisfactory outcome Mr Evans quarrelled with his natural father and the latter asked him not to visit them again. As with Mr Craig, this adoptee's criticisms of his natural father sounded almost exactly similar to those about his adoptive parents. He was critical of his father for not being more understanding and for not helping him to become more confident. At times it was difficult to distinguish whether he was referring to his natural father or to his adoptive father because of the close similarity of his views about the two. In spite of the developments following the meeting he maintained that he was glad of the opportunity to see his father in person. When last seen he was planning to trace his original mother, hoping that she would be the one to understand him.

Mr McLeod, a single man, came to know of his adoption in his late teens. He felt he had a fairly happy home but wished his parents had told him earlier and especially that they had shared more information about his background. From his account it sounded as if he and his mother were fairly dependent on each other, whilst the father was a more shadowy figure. Once told about his adoption in adolescence he became 'obsessed' about his biological background and whom he belonged to. A few years later both his parents died in quick succession and he especially missed his mother. At this stage his urge to discover his genealogical background became very strong: 'I wanted to know who I was and to meet my mother because she was my mother; blood, I felt, is thicker than water.' He visited the address he obtained from Register House and there he met his original maternal grandmother. She was apparently glad to see him and she put him in touch with the natural mother. The grandmother warned him to be careful because his existence was unknown to his mother's husband. The grandmother eventually arranged for them to meet in a café. He was surprised at the mother's youth compared to the age of his adoptive mother who was over forty at placement. Moreover, he was generally disappointed because the natural mother was not the woman he had imagined or hoped her to be:

Soon after we met I realised I was in for a great
disappointment; she was not what I imagined her to be and
she was not the plump, jovial and extrovert adoptive mother
that I had. She looked too reserved and no warmth came from
her. Her dyed hair and nails made her look common and I was
put off. I enjoyed meeting her though and she said she enjoyed
it too. She told me that when she first heard about me she had
a couple of sleepless nights because her husband did not know
and she couldn't tell him. After that we arranged to meet again,
though I was not really keen after the first encounter. I never
felt after the first meeting that I wanted to meet her a second
time . . . So the second time I did not turn up. She wrote
to me twice but I did not reply. She was a strange person to me

and she meant nothing. I heard later that she emigrated to Australia; I am glad I met her as I know now and don't have to wonder. I don't think that blood is thicker than water any more . . . it meant nothing to me anyway.

It is a fair assumption to make that this adoptee was trying to recapture, through his natural mother, the close relationship he had had with his adoptive one and whose loss he had not fully accepted. At one stage in the interview he described his attachment to older women, similar in build and temperament to his adoptive mother. The physical existence of a first mother perhaps makes it difficult for some adoptees to accept the death of the second before they have satisfied themselves that the original one is a different person. In the first two cases described all the negative aspects of the adoptive relationship were transferred onto the natural parent, whilst in the third one, the natural parent could not match up to the good qualities of the deceased adoptive parent. All three cases had one thing in common in that none of the natural parents matched up to the adoptees' images and expectations of them.

Mrs McKay lost both her parents when she was twenty and felt at the time very lonely and lost. Though she claimed that her adoption was not a satisfactory one she was surprised to find how much she missed her parents when they died. Before her adoption she had been in a children's home until the age of four. She had vague memories of that earlier life but her adoptive family used to answer questions as if she were theirs. At eleven, and after considerable pressure from herself, her mother admitted that she was their adopted child and told her that her real parents were dead. Some months after the parents' death the adoptee obtained the usual information from Register House and went to visit the address where her birth-mother had lived. Once in the neighbourhood she vaguely remembered places and from a corner shop she obtained information about her mother's present whereabouts. When she visited the address her natural mother recognised her at first sight and is reported to have said: 'I expected this for some time'. The mother had married the adoptee's real father a short time after the adoption went through. Both natural parents claimed to have made many unsuccessful efforts to have her back: 'My mother cried a lot when we met and she was trying to tell me how much she and my father wanted me, but that they couldn't cope at the time. They kept saying that they have a lot to make up to me. I suppose they felt very bad.' For the past year now this adoptee and her natural parents have been meeting frequently. She claims to be much happier as a person compared with what she was before and that her natural parents are very glad to see her too. Occasionally she wonders if she has been disloyal towards her adoptive family and she feels bad and guilty. Though when first interviewed she was very critical of her adoptive mother, after the meeting with her real parents she almost came to idealise the adopted one.

Seven more adoptees located various blood relations but only in one case was an ongoing relationship established. In spite of her wish 'not to descend' on her original mother's address without prior arrangement, Miss Smith did exactly this. She could think of no other way. At the supplied address she met a maternal aunt and various cousins who talked to her extensively about her natural mother. They also gave her details of her mother's illness and subsequent death soon after she had given birth to her:

I was previously told that my mother had died at my birth but I couldn't believe it. I have no doubt now, but since I found out for myself I feel so much calmer. I also know that there is nothing more to be done, but I am very glad I met at least somebody who knew her and who could talk to me about her and show me photographs of her. I am so glad I could do this . . . In a way I was also pleased to find that what my parents told me was true.

This adoptee had focused all her differences and disagreements with her adoptive family on her adoptive status and she had convinced herself that the only solution to her problems was to find her natural mother to whom she was feeling closer, at least in fantasy. After she was faced with the reality of her natural mother's death and had heard a lot of detail about her as a person, she sounded at a subsequent contact, more reconciled and was seeing her differences with her parents in a different perspective.

Mrs Drummond was eventually able to contact a cousin of her original mother. The latter talked to her about her mother and provided her also with an early photograph. However, the cousin refused to disclose the mother's address until she had time to discuss the suggestion with her. The cousin's description and the photograph seemed to fire the adoptee's imagination more and the wish for a meeting became a constant preoccupation:

> I think she sounds a delightful person. She really sounds a
> kind, warm-hearted person. She sounds exactly what I have
> been looking for. I learned also that she is not married and there
> is a very good chance that we will be able to do something for
> each other. A photograph is not enough; it does not give you
> what you really want; it is only a photograph.

When the adoptees' desire to meet the original parents is very strong and the stakes on such a meeting high, then usually no amount of background information supplied at this late stage will suffice.

Two other adoptees were successful in locating a sibling who acted as a go-between for the adoptees and their mothers but the latter seemed reluctant to agree to a meeting. In the first case, a very unhappy young woman, who was feeling isolated and unwanted, managed to trace a half-blood-brother. They established contact and she found him a great comfort. Through this brother, she traced her original mother in London, but the latter refused to see her or have anything to do with her. The adoptee felt rejected and unwanted but was still hoping that her mother would change her mind. She talked of her need to be mothered and as a last resort she hoped her birth-mother would at least consent to speak to her on the telephone. The brother's explanations about her unrealistic expectations from their mother would not dissuade her: 'It is too late to give her up now after waiting for so many years. If I give her up now who do I turn to . . .?' With someone as unhappy as this particular adoptee, who had built up so many expectations, perhaps only the introduction of reality could be of some help.

Mr Simpson succeeded in tracing an aunt from whom he learned a fair amount about his original mother's current circumstances. In spite of explanations from the aunt that it was not advisable to meet his mother, he was quite insistent about it. He wanted to hear from her why she gave him up and whether she wanted him before doing so. He said that his motives for the meeting were rather punitive and his mother's reluctance to see him increased both his anger and determination to do so: 'I want to see her for myself and confront her with the "why". I would still want to know even if I found that my parents were evil. I want to see for myself. Unless I meet her I will not settle down or rest.' When seen on a second occasion, four months later, he appeared more reasonable and understanding and he had now given up the idea of meeting her. He implied that the various discussions he had had on the matter had convinced him of the futility of any further attempts. He felt satisfied with what he already found out. At this point he started also to view his relationship with his adoptive family in a slightly more positive light. Talking things over in the course of this study seemed to help some adoptees to clarify their feelings and their position.

How helpful to the adoptees was the search?

Irrespective of their immediate reaction to the amount and type of information obtained, eight out of ten adoptees had no regrets about the steps they had taken. Adoptees in both the Meet the Natural Parents group and the Background Information group felt in their majority (80 per cent) that the results of their enquiry were 'helpful' or of 'some help' to them. The remaining 20 per cent were either unsure or were certain that it was of 'no help' and they wished they had not embarked on it.

Helpful

Adoptees in this group made comments which indicated that their efforts had brought them some contentment or satisfaction, even if their ultimate goals had not yet been achieved. They talked of 'knowing where I stand', being 'more at peace with myself', 'contented', 'much happier', having 'bridged the gap', or 'it brought me a lot of comfort'. One young mother remarked: 'Even if I do not succeed in meeting my mother, I feel much better having got a birth certificate with something real on it about myself; it is something of my own and of me; it is me.'

One male adoptee wanted to stress how the information he obtained helped him to establish who he is. He wished—like many others—that there was similar information about the natural father: 'It could have helped me to complete myself.' A young teenager felt quite pleased and almost exhilarated with the information:

When at school the other children used to say, 'I was born in such and such a place', but I could never really tell them where I was born. Some children knew I was adopted and they would challenge me to say where I was born and they would laugh at me because I couldn't tell. Now I know . . . oh, it's a funny feeling; I feel as if I have got rid of a barrier or a wall and now I feel an awful lot easier in myself.

Miss Banks felt 'definitely better' since she found out more about her background: 'I know more about myself now than I did before and I feel much better.' One adoptee felt the search helped him to put together 'some missing links', whilst another did not now feel that he was 'cut off dead' from his origins. Mr Wolfe, who had been troubled about his origins since he found out at fifteen, said that he felt more content now because he knew where to put 'the ends of a string that were hanging out'. Mr Davidson, now in his early thirties, felt happier within himself and added, 'I don't think as much about it now as I used to.' Other adoptees were glad because they had established the 'truth' even though this had sometimes exposed their adoptive parents who had given them incorrect information:

I now know my real name and where I was born and something about my people. I was shocked at first to find that it didn't tie up with what my parents told me, but at least I know this is the truth and what I found is of great comfort to me.

Mrs Murray, who was at first upset to find that her natural mother was only a grocer's assistant, remarked: 'At least this is something more real than all my previous speculations. It gives you a jolt at first, but somehow you feel less restless later.'

Though most of the adoptees who had contact with a birth-parent or a relative were disappointed that their ultimate expectations were not fulfilled, nevertheless they felt that finding out and testing reality was a great help to them: 'I feel more at peace with myself', said one of them and another, 'I know where I stand', and a third, 'I seem to have matured through this process.'

The fact that these adoptees were feeling 'happier' or 'more content' or 'more at ease' with themselves did not necessarily imply that some of the general pressures they had been experiencing before were suddenly eliminated or had disappeared. There was a feeling of now having something tangible and more real on which to base their general outlook and thinking. On the whole more satisfaction was expressed by those who set out to obtain information than by those who were searching for a parent.

Some adoptees who were searching for their original parents and who were either unsuccessful or found out some painful facts, reacted in two ways: either they continued the search or they became very critical of the legal provision and wanted to see it abolished. It was mostly unhappiness and desperation which kept many of these searching; indeed the process itself seemed to protect them from their loneliness and distress.

Unhelpful

One in every five adoptees, mostly those searching for a birth-parent, was either uncertain of the value of the information obtained or certain that it contributed to increased 'restlessness' and 'un-happiness'. Some of this group were in favour of discontinuing this legal right. They gave as reasons for their feelings either the 'un-palatable' facts they had found out or that the information, especially the address, stimulated more curiosity and they could not stop searching.

These adoptees were mostly very unhappy and insecure people who felt lost after the search because their difficulties were still with them. They became critical of and angry with whoever they thought contributed to their distress. This included natural and adoptive parents and the system of adoption as well as the right to search out their origins.

Their comments were characteristic of their anguish and anger: 'It is better to live in oblivion and not know'; or, 'abolish the system altogether'; or, 'all single mothers should be aborted'; or, 'no mother should ever be allowed to give up her child'; or, 'it is the authorities who are to be blamed for not selecting better adoptive parents'. This latter point was strongly made by a number of adoptees who perceived their adoptions as unsatisfactory.

I would like to know the names of my parents, or at least
of my mother, where and when I was born and their
occupations. Also what kind of people my mother and father
were, what hobbies they had, whether they were friendly people
and what likes and dislikes they had. Above all why she was
giving me up and whether I was wanted before I was given
up . . .

> Female adoptee

Adoptees had important views about the present system and its
provision which enabled them to obtain access to their original
birth entry. They also had views about the timing of the adoption
revelation, how parents should tell their children they are adopted
and what type of background and genealogical information is
desirable.

Views about the current Scottish system

Seven out of every ten adoptees would like the present system, by
which an adopted person can obtain a copy of his original birth
entry, to be retained and improved. Almost one-quarter wanted
to see the present system retained without the revelation of addresses.
These responses were all made by adoptees who were searching for
background information. Only four adoptees (or 6 per cent) were in
favour of abolishing the present system altogether.

Four-fifths of the adoptees in the study set out to obtain information thinking that this was their 'birthright' rather than a unique
provision of the Scottish law. Consequently they saw any attempt to
withdraw this facility as an attack on adopted people, or as depriving
them of fundamental information about their origins. The comments
of the more articulate adoptees were representative of the feelings
of the rest:

I think that you have got a right to seek out that information,
as long as you do not abuse the privacy of the other person . . .

the whole thing shouldn't be coated in further mystery. I don't think anyone has a right to withhold it from adopted people, provided they are of an adult age . . . It is the freedom of the individual involved . . .

Another adoptee remarked that it would be unfair to stop adoptees obtaining even this sketchy bit of information which can be of such a great comfort to them.

You cannot always rely on your parents to give you the information you want. Not to have such a basic human right is depriving someone of his civil liberties . . . I don't think that many people bother to go and find out about it because they don't need to, but adopted people should be entitled to know what stock they come from. If you are not adopted you know who your parents are, but if you are adopted that means there is always something about you that you don't know and I think you should. Not because you want to go and live with your natural parents, but because without this information you cannot be a whole person.

Other adoptees remarked that 'no one has a right to cut off your roots', or, 'if I had come up against a blank wall in my enquiries I think I would go mad'; 'your origins are yours and nobody should deny you access to information'; 'one should be allowed to find out to fill the gaps that are there.'

When it was pointed out to adoptees that their original parent(s) made a decision to relinquish them permanently and that it might be hard on them to feel they could be followed twenty or thirty years later, they generally showed considerable understanding. Most of them thought that it was fair for both parties to have equal rights in this respect. In other words that both the adoptee and his original parents should have the right to meet later in life if they all wished such a meeting. The address of neither party should be divulged, but the agency that arranged the adoption should take the responsibility of establishing the wishes of both parties. Adoptees were ready to accept that no agency could keep track of people's movements, unless they still resided at their original addresses. One adoptee who had already done a lot to find her was insistent that her mother should be given the choice:

I think that my mother should quietly and discreetly be given the choice to see me or not. If she says 'no' well that's it. I

143

wouldn't hurt her in any way. I feel she has been hurt enough
. . . I think that all these years, it's a thing that happened to
her and she can't forget it, but I think she ought to be given
the chance by a third party, an agency or an information bureau.
If I were told that the shock would be tremendous for her I
wouldn't do it.

Other adoptees were clear in their minds that the wishes of the
natural parent should first be established by a third party, such as
an adoption agency. One of them added, however:

I think the danger is when you get people who are emotionally
unsettled and have either a dream child or a dream parent and
chase after what is really a will-o'-the-wisp and they get an
awful shake when they come up against the truth . . . sometimes
of course you don't know whether it is better for them to get
this shake for their own self, but it may not be for the sake of
the other person . . .

The young student teacher again:

Everybody ought to know and find out what they like. If they
have any intention of finding their parents, there should be
somebody there to explain . . . not just barge on, be very careful
and tactful if it were possible to get in touch. The most tactful
way possible to protect both parties. Perhaps a third person
or an agency should act as an intermediary.

Timing of the adoption revelation

The adoptees had no definite views about the exact timing of telling.
The attitude was perhaps a confirmation of earlier finding, that
'telling' by itself is of secondary importance and only meaningful
when seen within the context of relationships. Most of them said,
'they must be told when still children', but they defined children as
being anything between four and twelve. Few specifically quoted
ages under five. They were all agreed, however, that the child should
be told by his own parents and on no account be left to find out
from outsiders or from documents. Those who found out from
outside sources and especially from other children felt very resentful.
Adoptees recognised that if you leave it till after the child starts
school then the possibility of learning from outside is greatly

increased but some still maintained that the ages between four and eight were the most appropriate for 'telling'. A factory labourer, who was critical of his now deceased parents for never revealing his adoption to him, thought that the ideal time was fourteen or fifteen. He only told his own step-daughter that he was not her real father when she was fifteen. He maintained that she did not mind learning at this late stage.

Another adoptee who was told by other children at the age of ten, and who was somewhat critical of his parents, recreated the same pattern with his own adopted son. He did not reveal his adoptive status to him until after he found out from other children also at the age of ten. Where the relationship between the adoptee and his parents was a 'good' one, little importance was usually attached to the timing of revelation unless it was left beyond the age of about ten.

There was a very small number of adoptees, four out of seventy, who wished they had never known. A young man who was told only at nineteen, wished he had never been told because he felt so different after that and had to reconsider his whole conception of himself. He added: 'Perhaps it would have been different if I was told when still a child'. By child he meant about the age of seven or eight. A young girl who was told before the age of five equally felt that 'there is a lot to be said about children not knowing . . . happiest to live in oblivion.' These were people, who for a number of reasons perceived themselves and their relationships as 'unhappy', seeing their adoptive status as being the prime reason for such feelings.

How the adoptees would like parents to tell their children they are adopted

Among adoption workers there is a fair amount of discussion as to whether adoptive parents should refer to the birth-mother as 'mother' or, for example, as the 'woman that gave birth to you'. This distinction, it is argued, would prevent children from feeling confused by having two sets of parents. The same group would like to reserve the word 'mother' and 'father' to the people who bring up the child denying that the word has any connection with the biological happening. In other words the biological happening of conception and birth should not be confused with real parenthood which involves the whole process of upbringing with its attendant relationships.

The adoptees in the study had no doubts or reservations about what to call the people who gave birth to them. They were their 'birth-mother' or 'birth-father' or 'birth-parents'; or 'my first mother', or 'my other parents'. But they were also unanimous that the real feeling was attached to the words 'mother' and 'father' when these were used in connection with their adoptive parents:

> These are your real parents; they are part of you; it is
> inconceivable to think of anybody else who is so meaningful
> to you . . . my first parents have quite a different meaning
> to me. They are part of my history and of my past. I need to
> know about them in order to understand myself . . .

These adoptees would have felt resentful if their first parents had been referred to other than as mother and father. 'It would be disrespectful', said one of them, 'to call them other than mother and father.' The adoptees saw no difficulty in accommodating two sets of parents if telling was done in a sensitive and truthful manner. They would like their parents to tell them in a way that did not make them feel ashamed of their past. They were clear that any explanation should follow the child's readiness to absorb information. Such information should be given simply, without inhibitions and embarrassment, which 'make you feel bad' or 'guilty'. They further explained that it was mostly between the ages of twelve and seventeen that they felt both curious and inquisitive about their origins. Adoptees appreciated genealogical information given earlier but it was during adolescence that they really came to feel the need to go over the facts again and to have details to satisfy their curiosity. Some, recognising their own and their parents' difficulty to raise the subject of adoption, suggested that it would have been of great help to have gone at this stage to the agency that arranged the adoption and be given information by a sympathetic person:

> It is not so much the particulars that matter but to be able to
> discuss your adoption with another person who is knowledgeable
> about the subject and who understands. It is difficult at this
> stage to raise awkward questions with your parents, especially if
> you don't have the habit of talking about things . . .

One of the main things adoptees in the study would have liked to hear was that their birth-parents wanted them or loved them and that they were not rejected. 'To carry the feeling of having been unwanted by your original parents', said one of them, 'is very heavy and can spoil your self-image for life.' Social workers working with unmarried mothers know what warm feelings they have for their children and how difficult they find it to part with them. It is only exceptionally that a mother, because of mental or social handicap, may appear blasé or in extreme cases may abandon her child. The social worker's ability to present the natural parents' positive image can help the adoptive parents to do the same with the child. The adoptive parents have a good opportunity to explain to the child in a simple way that his first parents loved him but could not keep him because of their circumstances, Some explanation of the circumstances could be helpful but again should follow the child's capacity to cope with realities like death (a rare phenomenon anyway). To be told that their mother's occupation, family circumstances or her awareness that they needed 'a full-time mother' and/or a father, were seen as acceptable explanations. The adoptees also liked to hear that they were 'chosen' or 'selected', as long as no fairy tales were built up around this; such comments made them feel wanted and proud. It may be difficult, however, for adoptive parents to say they chose the child when in the present day reality of adoption practice no such choice is exercised beyond a general preference for a particular sex, age and perhaps colour. Adoptees were ready to accept this, adding that adoptive parents could find other ways of transmitting feeling and information that can make adopted children feel 'special' as natural children feel special to their parents. They were aware that a feeling of belonging and pride in oneself does not come from certain words but from the totality of relationships and the feeling behind what is said. This kind of outlook held by many adoptees further confirmed the study's findings that the actual telling was of secondary importance to the quality of family relationships.

Occasional 'unsavoury' facts about criminality or promiscuity in the child's genealogy have little or nothing to do with the natural parents' feelings towards a child or about how a child will grow up in his adoptive home. The adoptees were interested to hear mostly about their parents' feelings towards them at the time and not to hear depreciative facts about them. Some authorities would obviously argue that it would not be helping the child to come to terms with reality if unpleasant facts about his original parents were withheld.

147

One adoptee's comment was that it would be unfair to harp on aspects of a parent's behaviour when the full circumstances behind it would not be explained or understood.

Adoption carries many hard realities about it and there is no reason to create or transmit hypothetical ones. As many adoptees remarked, it is the aspect of illegitimacy that worries them most, rather than adoption. Most of the adoptive parents concealed it or went to great lengths to explain that the original parents were married, when this was not in fact so. The adoptees would not like this kind of cushioning and would appreciate, they said, the truth about their status and that of their first parents. But they stressed again that this information should be given gradually to take account of the child's understanding, to avoid anxieties and the build-up of unpleasant fantasies. Almost all parents who surrender their children do so because father and mother do not live together. This makes it difficult for them to offer the child a real home and is a major factor in deciding to surrender the child to another family. Later on, preferably in early adolescence, the child may be told that his parents were not legally married. The adoptive parents' own attitude towards illegitimacy and unmarried parenthood can be important in the amount of acceptance, tolerance and under-standing they can convey. Illegitimacy, which is a man-made distinction, is not something transmitted from parents to children. Parental anxieties, however, about an adopted child's illegitimacy or social background portray a biological determinism and a lack of confidence in their own importance in shaping their child's life.

Adopted children also, like other children, like to know and talk about sex. The revelation of adoption may follow from a talk about sex or the other way round. Adoptive parents should explain both matters in simple terms which their child can grasp. More compli-cated information can be given later on, to take account of the child's understanding. The study has shown that often difficulty in talking about the adoptive status was accompanied by difficulties in talking about sex. It would be hard for parents to talk about adoption without reference to sex and subsequently to the fact that the child was illegitimate or that his parents did not live together.

Background information desired

The adoptees desired full background information about their

148

origins and genealogy. They maintained that the existence of such material would make it unnecessary for many of them to pursue contact with their natural parents. Ideally they would like all relevant background information to be passed on to the adoptive parents who would in turn pass it on to the children. They felt, however, that there would always be certain adoptive parents who would find it difficult to share or who would find themselves unable to reveal the adoptive status. 'It is not satisfactory', many argued, 'to leave it all to the adoptive parents. There is no guarantee that they will either retain the information or share it.' There will also be many situations in which, by the time the adoptee is interested enough in his origin, or able to grasp certain facts, the adoptive parents may be dead or not available for comment and clarification. As stated earlier, many adoptees are motivated to search out their genealogical background after the death of one or both parents. Having somewhere to go and clarify their origins, at a time when some may feel alone, may help them to accept their recent loss.

The adoptees stressed the need for information about *both* natural parents and possible siblings. They saw the agency that arranged the adoption as the one which should be responsible for collecting and keeping the information. Furthermore, the full birth certificate should give the name of the agency that arranged the adoption so that adoptees would know where to go, when necessary. Some adoptees said they would have liked an experienced and understanding person with whom to talk about their situation and to reflect on it.

Most of them felt that it was very difficult for non-adopted people to really understand them or enter into their feelings. They perceived themselves as being different and considered that only someone who was also different in some way could understand them. The writer was often told, 'You will not understand but others adopted like myself would'; or, 'I do not expect you to understand my feelings because you can't know what it feels like . . .' One adoptee, however, remarked: 'You will understand me because you are different, too.' When I asked in what way was I different, she replied, 'You must know what it is to be different because you are a foreigner.' This example is given to illustrate some adoptees' need for considerable understanding. For reasons explained earlier, some came to feel 'inferior', 'unwanted', 'being different' or 'not whole persons' and an agency worker with the responsibility of sharing with them information about their background must appreciate this. Sensitive and knowledgeable handling at this stage may determine how well or otherwise the adoptee copes with this very personal and complex situation that often defies full understanding.

Not every adoptee wanted the same information but their comments as a whole pointed to the kind of information agencies should be collecting at the time the placement is being arranged. Experience suggests that when it is explained to the natural mother why it is necessary to obtain certain information about herself and the child's father, it is very unusual for her not to co-operate. In a recent study of mothers giving up their children, the writer noted their strong maternal feelings and their earnest desire to do anything possible to facilitate their child's future happiness. If information from agency records is often lacking it is not because of the mother's reluctance to co-operate, but usually the result of agency workers neglecting to collect and store vital information.

Adoptive couples, because of their dependency on the adoption agency which holds the resources (i.e., the babies), are unlikely to make demands and insist on being given full background information about the child and its origins. The onus should therefore be on the agencies to collate and give such information to the adoptive parents, preferably in writing. Memories fade over the years and information can be distorted.

Quotations from the adoptees' comments give a good indication of the type of information desired. The following quotation is from a midwife:

> I would like to know the names of my parents, or at least of my mother, where and when I was born and their occupations. Also what kind of people my mother and father were like—what hobbies they had, whether they were friendly people and what likings and dislikes they had. Above all why she was giving me up and whether I was wanted before I was given up. Photos would be of no value—they don't tell you much, for one thing they would be twenty years old now. You think of your mother more in terms of the time you were born . . . probably you will be shocked to find she is much older now . . .

A factory worker gave up his original wish to trace his mother after hearing about her extensively from a blood relation. He was

now clearer in his own mind about the type of information he would
have liked his adoptive parents or an agency to give him:

> The adoption society could collect information such as: why
> this adoption, why is the child given up and was the child
> wanted; what sort of person is the mother and the father; were
> they married; did they have other children; information about
> your grandparents too. If you could get this information without
> having to contact the original parent, then this would solve
> the problem. It would have solved the problem for me if I had
> been able to get this information from my adoptive parents.

Mr Tait commented that he would have liked to know who he
belonged to originally, the circumstances of his adoption, what
kind of people his natural parents were and what their situation was:
'Even such a basic thing as where you come from makes you feel
better'. Another adoptee remarked that adopted children like to have
information that helps them build their respective 'family trees'
and 'recognise themselves'. Miss Spears, the receptionist, added
among other things: 'Adopted children like to know where their
origins started; it adds to their personalities and it makes them feel
less different and more like everybody else'.

Some adoptees placed greater importance on factual type of
information:

> You want to know if they were black or fair haired, blue eyed
> or green eyed. What jobs they did. Which part of the country
> they come from. Whether they had any hobbies—I am musically
> minded myself and I often wonder if I have taken it from my
> natural parents . . . I would also like their names and ages.
> Where they were brought up and where I was born . . . I often
> walk in the street looking at people and thinking, 'Well, could
> she be my mother?' It arises from the fact that you don't know
> who you are. Maybe if it were not left until I was twenty before
> I was told, I might be feeling differently.

Two adoptees who were concerned, one about her own health
and the other about her child's, would have liked to have relevant
medical histories relating to any possible hereditary or congenital
conditions.

The young copyist said that she would have been satisfied and

151

perhaps not started her search at all if a lot of information about her genealogical background had been supplied to her:

> I probably wouldn't even want to meet my mother if I had information about her character and that of my father; the circumstances of the adoption and why; if I had any brothers and sisters; what sort of people my foreparents were and what kind of background. This could give me an idea of what sort of life I might have lived if I hadn't been adopted.

'A name and address', one adoptee remarked, 'means nothing; there's nothing you can do with it. You want information that brings people to life to help you build a true picture of your origins.'

Though the physical appearance of the original parents was not important to all adoptees, for some it assumed considerable significance. They saw information of this nature as being necessary to develop a self body-image and also to attach a distinctiveness to their children. 'If I had some description of my birth parents,' remarked one adoptee, 'it might help me to recognise myself.' Another added:

> You have no one to compare yourself with or to say, 'I took a bit after my father or after my grandmother . . .'; if I could just have a glimpse of my mother from a distance I would be satisfied. I don't want to disturb her, but just to look at her. Otherwise I will remain a stranger to myself . . .

Some adoptees would have been satisfied with a physical description or with a photograph whilst others, at this stage, thought that there was no substitute for a physical meeting. The difference between this group and those who wanted to see the parents in person was one of degree. The greater the problem of identity the greater the need to meet the parent in person. The less such problems existed the less the need for a meeting; they would have been satisfied with a description of the physical characteristics or with a photograph: 'I am more interested in what she looks like than what I am going to ask her. It's funny but I want to see me in her. It is important to me to find out who I took after'.

Certain adoptees implied that they were unable to hold the images of their children without knowing what their birth-parents looked like and who they and their children took after: 'Not knowing who I took after and what my natural parents looked like, I tend to see my children as part of my husband's family and much less as part of me.' Mrs McClure, the wife of a trader, remarked:

> My first child was a boy and my husband's relatives kept saying, oh! he is so much like his father or grandfather . . . and I felt very alone because I have nobody of my own to say, oh! he is like my father or like my mother and this is a terrible thing. Unless you have experienced this you do not realise how deep this feeling is . . . so I have been thinking of finding more about my natural father, especially since I became a parent . . .

Another adoptee, who would have been satisfied with a description of her natural parents, talked about her envy when her in-laws compared her children with their side of the family:

> You have them saying, he is like his grandfather or she takes after your cousin . . . Well, I can't say that and I do feel it deeply . . . sometimes it amuses me that my in-laws always find some resemblance between my children and their side of the family but never to any of mine . . . it has not occurred to my mother that this can hurt; my aunt is more considerate about this and is careful not to hurt my feelings.

In summary, the adoptees in the study made suggestions about the value of the current system, the timing and method of telling and the type of information they would ideally like to have, preferably from their parents. They would not be satisfied with generalities but with specific descriptive details that help to individualise the person. For example, it would not be sufficient to say that the father was a sportsman or a musician; they would like to know what sport, what kind of music or instrument. They saw the period of adolescence as the one during which they would have liked discussion of information given earlier or the revelation of further genealogical details.

The main aim of the study was to establish the past and current circumstances of adopted people who sought information about their origins and to examine their motivation for the search, their needs and general outlook. Adoptees in Scotland can usually expect to obtain from official records information about where and when they were born, who their original parents were and where they lived and what the occupation of the father or mother was at the time of birth. Because most adopted children are illegitimate, it is seldom that information about the father is available.

Each year only, a very small number of adopted people feel the impulse to seek out this type of genealogical information. Because most of those featuring in the study embarked on their search without prior knowledge of their special right, it can be assumed that if other adoptees felt the same need they would have done likewise. For the vast number of adoptees the impulse to search was in response to some deeply felt psychological need and rarely to a matter-of-fact attitude.

Two groups of adoptees were identified whose stated search-goals differed from the start. The goal of the first group was to find one or both of their natural parents whilst that of the second was to obtain background genealogical information. The two groups differed from each other in a number of ways, thus affording an opportunity not only for comparison but especially for gaining certain insights into the feelings, thinking and general needs of adopted people and in particular of those preoccupied with their origins. The adoptees who wanted to meet their natural parents were far more strongly motivated and more determined than those interested only in background information.

The adoptees in the sample came from different parts of the country and some were living outside Scotland at the time of the enquiry. A small number referred to their adoptive parents as foster parents, the word 'adoptive' not being much in use in their areas for this form of substitute parent-child relationship. This lack of differentiation between adoption and foster care could easily lead

154

to misunderstandings where social workers were selecting families to act as foster parents, rather than as adoptive ones.

A very high percentage of adoptees in the sample came to know about their adoptive status well after the age usually recommended by the literature on adoption. Three out of every five were told or found out after the age of ten. The later parents postponed the revelation the greater the possibility that the adoptee would find out from outside sources. In the absence of a control sample it is difficult to say whether adoptees who do not search into their original background are told at an earlier or at a similar stage. The fact that a great number of adoptees came to know about their adoptive status during adolescence and after made it possible for the study to reflect on certain developments in their lives that could not have been complicated by the knowledge of adoption.

Though the stage of 'telling' did not seem to be of paramount importance, adoptees who were told when under the age of ten were the more satisfied and the reverse was true of those who were told later. The majority of the adoptees thought that the age of four to eight was the most appropriate for 'telling'. Finding out from outside sources was strongly resented and the parents' reluctance to tell was bitterly criticised. Those who found out late or came to know about their adoption from outside sources were the most hurt and upset. It shook the faith of many of them in their parents and where it was accompanied by other adverse experiences within the family, irreparable damage was caused to the relationship between the adoptee and his parents.

The general reaction to being told by or finding out from outside sources, especially in adolescence and adult life, was mostly painful and distressing. On the basis of the adoptees' comments the view was formed that adoption is felt as a form of abandonment or rejection irrespective of the quality of other experiences. When knowledge of adoption is delayed till adolescence or adult age, the feeling of 'rejection' seems to be infinitely greater than when revelation takes place in earlier years. It appears that when knowledge of adoption comes early—possibly before the age of eight or ten—there is time for the trauma to heal where accepting and cherishing relationships prevail. The scar, however, appears to remain for ever and is liable to open up under extreme forms of stress. When knowledge of adoption is delayed till adolescence and beyond, the possibility of a healing process is considerably diminished.

Among adoptees the initial reaction to late discovery of the adoption situation was one of shock and stunned numbness. Later it was followed by grief accompanied by intense criticism and anger towards the parents for holding back. The adoptees' grief took the form of directing most of their thoughts and feelings to objects or information associated with their birth-parents but especially the mother. The process of grief seemed difficult for many because they had no, or very little, information about the 'lost' set of parents to whom to attach the feeling.

Adoptees, who were told at some time below the age of eleven, could not remember reacting so strongly or painfully at the time except where the revelation took a destructive and vindictive form. Otherwise some parents were able to transmit through 'telling' a feeling of pride and well-being which the adoptees valued immensely. When the meaning of adoption, i.e., 'surrender' and 'loss', started to seep in a kind of retrospective thinking and grieving began, it was far more manageable compared with those who only came to know about their adoption in their teens or later.

There was a general reluctance among adoptive parents to reveal or share information about the child's original genealogy and also how he came to be adopted. Though this attitude, as well as the reluctance to reveal the adoptive situation at all, had some cultural sanction in certain parts of the country, in most other cases information was deliberately withheld because of the parents' fears and anxieties. The adoptees interpreted their parents' failure to share with them as reflecting a lack of trust and precariously built relationships. Many regretted the fact that 'telling' about adoption and gradually sharing information was not used as an opportunity to develop and cement family relationships. Though some adoptees were prepared to recognise that their parents withheld or distorted certain particulars because they wanted to protect them, they still maintained that truth and honesty would have helped to enhance their respect for them. It would have been easier, they argued, to come to terms with painful facts about themselves than to live with lies and have their trust in their parents shaken. Secrecy and evasiveness gave many the feeling that adoption was something shameful or not the done thing. This feeling, which was often reinforced by community attitudes, contributed to the development of a poor self-image and to a reluctance among adoptees to reveal their adoption even to people very close to them.

Adoptees who were given no information about their background, or to whom some information was disclosed but in a hostile way which was often depreciative of the natural parents, were generally keen to find their birth-parents. Their total attention and impulses were in this direction. In contrast, those who were told something positive about their natural parents, were now mostly inclined to search for additional information about their genealogical background. Similarly, where the adoptees had some knowledge about their origins the strength of their motivation for the search was weak. The opposite was true in cases where there was a lack of such information.

There was a stage in the adoptees' life, mostly before the age of about eleven, when they did not seem particularly interested to talk about their adoption and in fact would not have welcomed frequent discussion. It was at the start of their early teens that they mostly found themselves desperately wanting to hear from their parents about their adoption, about their origins and about their first set of parents. This need reached its climax in adolescence and it appeared to be closely associated with the adoptees' efforts to establish their identity as individuals, wanting at the same time to integrate their first parents into their system in order to feel more complete. Satisfaction of this need at the adolescent stage, the adoptees maintained, would have helped them to understand themselves and other people better and possibly to forestall their subsequent preoccupation with their first set of parents. The adoptees were quite clear, however, that some preoccupation with one's origins never stops except with death.

It was a characteristic of most of the families in which there was little or no communication about the adoption situation, that there was a lack of communication about other things as well. For some families this reflected a traditional pattern of functioning, whilst for others it was the result of 'family malfunctioning'. Whilst the former was mostly a characteristic of working-class families the latter transcended social class barriers. In both instances the adoptees felt deprived of what they saw as their birthright to know. Though almost all the adoptees were emphatic that both telling and the sharing of detailed information were of great importance, they also conveyed the view that these aspects were meaningless unless seen in the context of the totality of life situations and experiences. Besides many adoptees' frustrations and criticisms about the

157

stage at which their adoptive status was revealed to them and about the kind of information they were given, there was a fundamental disappointment in the quality of their family relationships. Many of them perceived their adoptive home life as unsatisfactory, lacking in feeling and warmth and as having failed to develop in them a sense of attachment, belonging and pride in being adopted. They did not meet with any form of discrimination in favour of other siblings within the adoptive home but claimed that their experiences of an unhappy home life were also shared by the parents' own children, where these existed. For the group of adoptees who experienced their adoptive home life as unsatisfactory, preoccupation with their adoptive home life took precedence over all other types of relationships, such as wife and husband or mother and child.

In a small number of cases, however, earlier 'good' relationships seemed to be distorted by recent events such as death of a parent, property disputes, illness etc. Many adoptees attributed their own unhappiness, sense of emptiness, isolation and sometimes distress to either the poor quality of their home life or to the fact of being adopted.

Where the adoptees' perception was generally of an unsatisfactory home life it was usually accompanied by a poor self-perception, too. Many had a negative image of themselves and talked of their inner 'void', their desolation and general incapacity to form meaningful relationships with other people. They felt ashamed and embarrassed at being adopted and illegitimate. A fair number of these had already received psychiatric treatment whilst others were in obvious need of such help. The search itself was helping many to keep themselves together and the process was assuming greater importance than the goal. Their main criticism of their home life was about the lack of emotional satisfactions, absence of warmth and failure to develop in them a sense of belonging. The greater the dissatisfaction with their family relationships and with themselves, the greater the possibility that they would now be searching for their original parents. The better their image of themselves and of their parents, the greater the possibility that they would be looking for background information.

Though adolescence was the most common period when the adoptees first thought of enquiring into their origins, it was some subsequent life crisis that eventually decided them to act. The most usual events that generated an impulse to search were death of one or both parents, illness, expectation of a child, pending marriage or separation or when inner pressures could no longer be contained. The most severe crises were precipitated by events which carried a sense of loss or abandonment, such as: death of a parent especially when followed by the re-marriage of the surviving one; separation from or desertion by a parent, husband, boy-friend or girl-friend. Crises of this nature seemed to affect worse those who were less well settled and more vulnerable. The current experience of loss appeared to re-awaken the 'rejection' or 'abandonment' felt through the loss of the first parents. The death of one or both adoptive parents was usually followed by a strong desire for the first set of parents, especially the mother, but its intensity varied depending on the quality of the adoptees' earlier home life.

The adoptees' expectations from the search were closely associated with the type and amount of information revealed, with the quality of their home life, the perception of themselves and with the nature of their current stress. Though all of them wanted to find answers to such questions as to who their natural parents were, why they were given up for adoption and whether their first set of parents wanted them and loved them, many were also hoping to develop a relationship of friendship with them. There was a hope that their natural parents would make up to them what they had missed from their earlier relationships. The ones who were mainly satisfied with their adoptive home life were looking for information that would help them to complete themselves, whilst the more disillusioned ones were hoping for nourishment from mainly the mother.

The outcome of the search left many adoptees with mixed feelings. Those who were looking for additional information were generally satisfied with the results but ideally they would have liked more detailed particulars. They were surprised to find the paucity of the official records which often did not go beyond what they already knew. Those who set out hoping to meet their parents were less satisfied. Though they welcomed what information they obtained they were mostly unsuccessful in their attempts to attain their main goal. After the initial search a very small number were thinking of giving up, but the rest, and these were mostly the ones who were feeling under the greatest pressure, were determined to go on. For them the search and its continuation seemed to protect them from their loneliness and unhappiness.

A very small number were eventually successful in finding a parent or a blood relation. With one exception, there was no indication that earlier expectations were fulfilled or relationships developed. Where a meeting occurred it was usually followed by some disillusionment in the adoptee with a tendency for the latter to transfer on to the original parents many feelings that were formerly held about the adoptive ones. The adoptees claimed, however, that following these contacts they found it easier to come to terms with their condition and circumstances.

Almost all the adoptees, irrespective of the objectives and outcome of their search, were in favour not only of retaining the system by which they were able to obtain information, but also of improving it. Their views and suggestions about how best to do this appear in Chapter 10.

In conclusion, the majority of adoptees searching into their genealogical background and especially most, but not all, of those trying to find their birth-parents were unhappy and lonely people and a considerable number had had psychiatric help. They generally hoped that the search would lead to new nurturing relationships or at least to the development of a more secure personality. A number of important factors jointly or separately seemed to combine to bring about the search for the natural parents. These were: the non-disclosure of background genealogical information or the revelation of only hostile particulars; unsatisfactory adoptive home relationships; a negative self-image; and having had psychiatric help. Late knowledge of adoption had no significant influence on the search goals (see Appendix: Table 11.1). A core of twenty-two adoptees in the Meet the Natural Parents group shared three important characteristics: the non-disclosure of background information or the revelation of only hostile particulars; unsatisfactory adoptive family relationships; and negative self-image. Only one adoptee in the Background Information group shared all these three characteristics.

The study identified three main areas which have important implications for adoption practice: the developing child's need for a warm, caring and secure family life; the adoptees' vulnerability to experiences of loss, rejection or abandonment; and the adopted persons need to know as much as possible about the circumstances of their adoption and about their genealogical background in order to integrate these facts into their developing personality.

160

The unhappiness and disillusionment of many adoptees who featured in the study was often associated with an emotionally sterile early family life which was later reinforced by other adverse life experiences. Being adopted, as such, did not appear to be the real cause for the breakdown of the personal relationships described. The adoptees wished for parents who were happily married, who could display their love and affection, making them feel secure and wanted. Provided that the home was a loving one and the child accepted for what it was, bringing up an adopted child did not seem to differ from rearing an own or any other child. This conclusion was mainly reached because the adoptive parents' attitude towards their own children (where these existed) did not differ from that towards the adopted ones. In other words, the parents' attitude towards their adopted children was a reflection of their general child rearing practices. A further observation pointing to this conclusion was the adoptees' varied coping with late revelation which was related more to their perception of the quality of their adoptive home life rather than to the stage of 'telling'.

The adoption situation itself presents three main tasks which, if badly managed, could complicate the child-parent relationship. Where this happens the likelihood is that the difficulties will be projected on to the adoption situation. The first task is the degree of the parents' acceptance of their own condition and of the reality of their adoptive parenthood, emotionally coming to accept and recognise the child as their own. The undue stress often laid on the differences between adoption and biological parenthood tends to create considerable guilt feelings among parents who want to see the child as their own and relate to it unconditionally. Whilst it is necessary for the parents to acknowledge the existence of the first set of parents, it is also imperative that at the same time they should come to feel that the child is rightfully theirs and to respond to it as if it were theirs by birth. After all, most of the adoptees interviewed said very clearly and definitely that though they knew they had a biological set of parents, it was to their adoptive mother and father that they responded as true parents and for whom they had real feelings. The words 'mother' and 'father' had emotional meaning only in relation to their adoptive parents and such feelings were evoked only in relation to them. They saw their adoptive parents as their true and rightful parents and even where the relationship failed, most of them still maintained very warm feelings for them.

If adopted children want, and try, to see their adoptive parents as their real parents, it also follows that successful parenting must involve the emotional acceptance of the children as one's own, without inhibition or guilt.

Whether adoption agencies can select homes which can offer such qualities as 'love', 'warmth' and 'acceptance' as outlined by the adoptees is debatable. These are all intangible qualities which are difficult to identify at the selection stage. Social workers and other similar professionals can reach only a limited level of agreement in their assessments of people and this makes any selection a precarious procedure. Interpretations of what is a 'warm', 'loving' and 'secure' couple can differ and are open to a fair amount of speculation and guesswork. It is even more difficult to identify with certainty the kind of attitudes at the selection stage which point to likely relationship difficulties later on. Even if it were possible to make accurate assessments at the selection stage, there would still be no guarantee that peoples' attitudes, needs and reactions would not change under the impact of new experiences which might affect the parent-child relationship. General statements at the selection stage regarding a couple's feelings about their childlessness and infertility are usually not indicative of future reactions to a real child. When applicants are under scrutiny and over-dependent on the agency, they are unlikely anyway to share their true feelings. More careful selection could have perhaps eliminated the most gross aspects of emotional and physical neglect the study came across but perhaps not the rest. Similarly the current practice of theoretical preparation for adoptive parenthood seems to be of limited value as it deals with the parents in isolation. Practice suggests that it is with the real experience of caring for a child that some couples may need help, and ideally they should then feel able to consult with the placing agency. It could be argued, however, that the current methods of selection with the stress on the authority of the agency and the dependence of the client, do not encourage adoptive couples to go back to the agency for consultation without feeling a failure.

The adopted person's vulnerability to experiences of loss, abandonment or rejection is mostly related to his feelings about being given up by his original parents. The degree of acceptance of this condition varies among adoptees. Later losses or serious crises or disappointments in life seem to reactivate such feelings. Yet again, where the adopted person had developed a feeling of well-being and belonging

162

later experiences of 'rejection' or 'loss' seemed to affect him less compared to those who did not come to feel in this way. Where the distress or unhappiness arising from such new experiences is focused on the adoption situation, the adoptee may be better helped by someone with knowledge and understanding of adoption.

Telling about adoption and sharing background information involves some very deep emotions on the part of the adopters and of the growing child. Irrespective of the adopters' readiness at selection stage to be honest and open with the child, when they are faced with the actual task some will find it difficult and will tend to postpone it until the child comes to find out from another source. This usually sets in motion a cycle of inhibitions, mistrust and speculation. For a number of reasons there will always be parents who will find themselves unable to cope with some of the tasks that are peculiar to the adoption situation, such as 'telling', the disclosure of information and the handling of adolescent behaviour which focuses difficulties on the adoption situation.

The various issues outlined above point to the obvious need for adoption agencies to see their work as part of an ongoing process rather than as a once and for all activity; in other words, to see adoption as part of a continuum and give equal emphasis to its different stages. The process of 'selection' will have to be seen as an opportunity for preparation and for mutual trust to be developed between the agency and the parents. The agency's general approach and the organisation of its adoption work will determine, to a large extent, how far parents and children alike will feel able to call at the agency for consultation and advice, if necessary. It is hoped that the adoption agency of the future will always be available to natural and adoptive parents, as well as to adopted children and adults. Consultative services to these groups should be built into the structure of each agency and be made available and accessible, without unnecessary barriers, secrecy and evasiveness.

→ In Chapter 10 there is a detailed discussion about the type of information that adoptees would ideally like to have about their origins and general background, including their natural parents' medical history. The study has also shown that adolescence is the most crucial period during which adoptees become intensely pre-occupied and curious about themselves and experience a strong urge to find out about their first pair of parents. They make a desperate attempt at this stage to complete themselves by integrating within

163

their system their two pairs of parents. If knowledge about the first pair of parents is not forthcoming, such integration may not take place or it may turn out to be very precarious and likely to collapse under stress. Most adoptive parents seem to respond appropriately to their children's questions about their first parents, without feeling threatened or anxious. As a long period elapses, however, between the stage at which agencies pass on information to the parents and the stage at which the latter have to share it with their children, it would be advisable for agencies to make it a practice to give all relevant background particulars in writing. In this way not only are memory failures avoided but also, and equally important, is the avoidance of misinterpretation or misperception of verbal information.

Irrespective of the approach suggested above, a minority of parents may still not find it easy to share what they know or they may be dead at the time when the adoptee is most curious to find out more. It is also not unusual for some adolescents to find it easier to accept information and advice from an outside source rather than from their own parents. For these reasons it is again important that the adopted person, and especially the adolescent, comes to know that he can go at any time to the agency that arranged his adoption and ask for details about his origins and why and how his adoption was arranged. There is no obvious reason why the agency should not respond to this need and discuss and share with the adoptee alone, or in his family's presence, information from its records. Such a service would require that every agency keeps a very detailed account about the circumstances and genealogy of each child it places. The law could also help by directing that the birth certificate should bear the address of the agency that made the original arrangements so that adoptees would know where to go. Adoption agencies by making themselves available, can be of great help not only to adoptees who happen to go through some crisis which they connect with their adoption, but also to some parents who find it difficult to cope with the child's repeated questions about his origins. The following extracts, from a letter addressed by a mother to her adoption worker, illustrate the latter point:

Dear . . .

I happened to have the radio on this morning when you were being interviewed . . . I was especially interested in the enquiry which is being made as to the advisability of adopted persons being allowed to find out from the register their parents' names . . . we feel quite strongly about this.

Bruce, on two or three occasions, asked who his 'other mummy' was and he found it very hard to believe that I did not know. On the last occasion, in desperation, I said that when he was grown up he could go to a big office in Edinburgh and find out for himself. Since then he has never mentioned the subject again.

We feel from our experience with our own adopted child that adopted children should be given the option of being able to trace their true mother . . .

Because of personality or of other special factors it is very possible that for a very small number of adoptees no amount of information or counselling will be of much help to them. They may see a meeting with their original parents as the only solution to their problems and in this respect the agency may have to exercise its judgment whether to act as a go-between for the child and his first parents. When a situation like this arises, perhaps only experienced reality can help people to come to some terms with their losses. This could eventually help them to emerge strengthened out of their isolation and distress. In an unpublished study by Triseliotis and Hall, the majority of mothers surrendering their children in Edinburgh in 1970 said they would not object to a future meeting between themselves and their child if this were suggested as necessary for their child's welfare and mental health.

The placing agency should ideally offer similar facilities and opportunities for counselling to the natural father or mother who, years later, may be focusing his or her possible unhappiness and guilt on the relinquishment of the child. In extreme cases the agency would again have to exercise its judgment whether a meeting between the original parent and the adoptee were advisable. For such an arrangement to take place it would be necessary for the adoptee to be adult enough to cope with this and for the agency to have prepared the ground well. So far, adoption agencies have only rarely known of natural parents calling years later to ask for news about a relinquished child.

The experience from Finland confirms most of our findings and recommendations. The main adoption agency there, which places about 225 children each year (45 per cent of the total adoptions in the country), provides for adoptees of any age calling in there to obtain background information about their biological parents. About fifty to seventy young people, mostly adolescents, go to the agency each year for information about their origins. Sometimes the initiative is taken by the adoptive parents who may call with the child. The service seems to have been of infinite benefit to the users without damage to the interests of other parties.[1]

The adoptees' quest for their origins was not a vindictive venture, but an attempt to understand themselves and their situation better. The contribution of the law and of adoption agencies towards such an objective can be of immense value to those who happen to feel in a limbo state. The self-perception of all of us is partly based on what our parents and ancestors have been, going back many generations. Adoptees, too, wish to base themselves not only on their adoptive parents, but also on what their original parents and forebears have been, going back many generations. It is the writer's view, based on his findings, that no person should be cut off from his origins.

Final note

The final report of the Departmental Committee on the Adoption of Children (Cmnd 5107) published in October 1972, made certain recommendations that give expression to the findings of this study. The report recommends that the adoption agency or, where there is no agency, the local authority, should be named on the adoption order, so that an adopted person may himself later be in a position to approach the agency for information that the adopters are unable or unwilling to provide. Furthermore, adoption agencies should be required to retain their records for seventy-five years. The committee also recommended that an adopted person aged eighteen years or over should be entitled to a copy of his original birth certificate. This recommendation would cover all adopted adults in England, Wales and Scotland.

Table 2.1 *Age at placement (n=70)*

Age	n	%
Under 3 months	30	43
3–6 months	12	17
7–12 months	2	3
12 months and over	16	23
Not known	10	14

Table 2.2 *Age of adoptive parents at placement (n=70)*

	Father *		Mother	
Age	n	%	n	%
Under 25	2	3	2	3
25–34	17	25	29	41
35–44	35	52	26	37
45 and over	13	20	13	19

* No fathers in three cases.

Table 3.1 *Age at adoption revelation and source of revelation (n=68)**

	Through parents	From other sources	Total	
Age	n	n	n	%
0–5 years	11	—	11	16
6–10 years	8	5	13	19
11–17 years	7	18	25	37
18–20 years	2	8	10	15
21 and over	2	7	9	13

* In this and subsequent tables two adoptees, whose search was unrelated to the two major goals of the rest, have not been included.

Table 3.2 *Knowledge of adoption related to search goals (n=68)*

	Goals				
	Meet the Nat/Parents		Background Information		Total
Knowledge of adoption	n	%	n	%	n
Before age 11	12	29	12	46	24
After age 10	30	71	14	54	44

Table 4.1   *Information revealed related to goals* (*n*=68)

	Goals			
	Meet the Nat/Parents		Background Information	
Information revealed	*n*	*%*	*n*	*%*
None or hostile	30	72	7	27
Some	11	26	9	35
Fair to considerable	1	2	10	38

Table 5.1   *The adoptees' perception of their adoptive home life related to the goals of their search* (*n*=68)

	Goals					
	Meet the Nat/Parents		Background Information		Total	
Relationships	*n*	*%*	*n*	*%*	*n*	*%*
Unsatisfactory	28	67	3	12	31	46
Fairly satisfactory	8	19	11	42	19	28
Satisfactory	6	14	12	46	18	26

Table 5.2   *The adoptees' perception of the quality of their adoptive home life related to the amount of background information revealed* (*n*=68)

	Information revealed			
	None or only hostile		Little to considerable	
Quality of relationships	*n*	*%*	*n*	*%*
Unsatisfactory	26	69	5	17
Fairly satisfactory	7	18	12	40
Satisfactory	5	13	13	43

Table 6.1   *The adoptees' self-perception related to their views about their home life* (*n*=68)

Quality of adoptive home relationships	Self-perception					
	Negative		Fairly negative		Mostly positive	
	n	*%*	*n*	*%*	*n*	*%*
Unsatisfactory	25	83	4	29	2	8
Fairly satisfactory	5	17	7	50	7	29
Satisfactory	—	—	3	21	15	63

Table 6.2 *The adoptees' self-perception related to their search goals* (*n*=68)

	Goals			
	Meet the Nat/Parents		Background Information	
Self-perception	*n*	*%*	*n*	*%*
Negative	25	60	5	19
Fairly negative	9	21	5	19
Mostly positive	8	19	16	62

Table 6.3 *Psychiatric help related to the perception of adoptive family relationships* (*n*=68)

	Psychiatric group		Non-psychiatric group	
Family relationships	*n*	*%*	*n*	*%*
Unsatisfactory	19	73	12	29
Fairly satisfactory	6	23	13	31
Satisfactory	1	4	17	40

Table 7.1 *Strength of motivation related to goals and self-perception* (*n*=68)

	Meet the Nat/Parents				Background Information			
	Self-perception				Self-perception			
	Negative or fairly negative		Mostly positive		Negative or fairly negative		Mostly positive	
Motivation	*n*	*%*	*n*	*%*	*n*	*%*	*n*	*%*
High	28	82	2	25	2	20	—	—
Medium	4	12	3	37	6	60	5	31
Low	2	6	3	38	2	20	11	69

Table 11.1   *Certain factors related to the adoptees' choice of goals* (*n*=68)

	Meet the Nat/Parents		Background Information		Total	
	n	%	*n*	%	*n*	%
1. *Knowledge of adoption*						
Before age 11	12	29	12	46	24	35
11 and after	30	71	14	54	44	65
2. *Information revealed*						
None or hostile	30	71	7	27	37	54
Little to						
considerable	12	29	19	73	31	46
3. *Perception of family relationships*						
Unsatisfactory	28	67	3	12	31	46
Fairly satisfactory						
to satisfactory	14	33	23	88	37	54
4. *Self-perception*						
Negative	25	60	5	19	30	44
Fairly positive						
to positive	17	40	21	81	38	56
5. *Psychiatric help*						
Psychiatric help	21	50	5	19	26	38
Others	21	50	21	81	42	62

Notes

Chapter 1

1 *Adoption of Children.*
2 J. G. Ansfield, *The Adopted Child.*
3 D. M. Schechter, 'Observations on adopted children', *Archives of General Psychiatry*, Vol. 3, July 1960, pp. 21–3.
4 L. Peller, 'About telling the child of his adoption', *Bulletin of the Philadelphia Association for Psycho-analysis*, Vol. 11, No. 4, December 1961, pp. 145–61; also, 'Further comments on adoption' in ibid., Vol. 13, No. 1, 1963, pp. 1–14.
5 H. D. Kirk, *Shared Fate*, pp. 43–6.
6 V. W. Bernard, 'Adoption' in Albert Deutsch and Helen Fishman (eds), *Encyclopedia of Mental Health*, Vol. 1, p. 103.
7 C. D. Krugman, 'Differences in the relation of children and parents to adoption', *Child Welfare*, Vol. 46, No. 5, 1967, pp. 267–72.
8 S. Freud, 'Family romance', in J. Strachey (ed.), *Collected Papers*, Vol. 5.
9 D. M. Schechter, P. Carlson, J. Q. Simmons and H. Work, 'Emotional problems in the adoptee', *Archives of General Psychiatry*, Vol. 10, 1964, pp. 109–18.
10 A. M. McWhinnie, *Adopted Children. How They Grow Up.*
11 F. Clothier, 'The psychology of the adopted child', *Mental Hygiene*, Vol. 27, 1943.
12 M. E. Schwartz, 'The family romance fantasy in children adopted in infancy', *Child Welfare*, Vol. 49, No. 7, 1970, pp. 386–91.
13 J. J. Lawton and Z. S. Gross, 'Review of psychiatric literature on adopted children', *Archives of General Psychiatry*, Vol. 11, 1964, pp. 635–44.
14 B. Kohlsaat and M. A. Johnson, 'Some suggestions for practice in infant adoption', *Social Casework*, Vol. 35, 1954, pp. 91–9.
15 J. Goodman, M. R. Silberstein and W. Mandell, 'Adopted children brought to child psychiatric clinics', *Archives of General Psychiatry*, Vol. 9, 1963, pp. 451–6.
16 H. D. Kirk, K. Johassohn and D. A. Fish, 'Are adopted children vulnerable to stress?', *Archives of General Psychiatry*, Vol. 14, 1966, p. 291.
17 N. Simon and A. Senturia, 'Adoption and psychiatric illness', *American Journal of Psychiatry*, Vol. 122, No. 8, 1966, pp. 858–68.
18 S. Reece and B. Levin, 'Psychiatric disturbances in adopted children: A descriptive study', *Social Work*, Vol. 13, No. 1, 1968, pp. 101–11.

171

Notes

19 M. Humphrey and C. Ounsted, 'Adoptive families referred for psychiatric advice: Part I. The children', *British Journal of Psychiatry*, Vol. 109, 1963, pp. 559–668.

20 B. Jaffe and D. Fanshel, *How They Fared in Adoption : A follow-up study*.

21 A. S. Elonen and M. E. Schwartz, 'A longitudinal study of the emotional, social and academic functioning of adopted children', *Child Welfare*, Vol. 48, No. 2, 1969.

22 L. H. Witmer, E. Herzog, E. A. Weinstein and M. E. Sullivan, *Independent Adoptions: A Follow-up Study*.

23 J. L. Hoopes, E. A. Sherman, E. A. Lawder, R. G. Andrews and K. D. Lower, *A Follow-up Study of Adoptions (Vol. 2): Post-placement functioning of adopted children*.

24 M. Bohman, *Adopted Children and their Families*.

25 R. R. Brenner, *A Follow-up Study of Adoptive Families*.

26 E. A. Lawder, K. D. Lower, R. G. Andrews, E. A. Sherman and J. G. Hill, *A Follow-up Study of Adoptions (Vol. 1): Post-placement functioning of adoptive families*.

27 P. Vodak *et al.*, *Problems Concerning the Adoption of Children*.

Chapter 2

1 J. Triseliotis, *Evaluation of Adoption Policy and Practice*.

2 A. M. McWhinnie, *Adopted Children: How They Grow Up*.

Chapter 3

1 H. Guntrip, *Schizoid Phenomena, Object Relations and the Self*, p. 267.

Chapter 4

1 J. Triseliotis, *Evaluation of Adoption Policy and Practice*.

Chapter 5

1 M. W. Gerard, *The Emotionally Disturbed Child*, pp. 12–14.

2 B. Jaffe and D. Fanshel, *How They Fared in Adoption: A follow-up study*.

Chapter 8

1 S. Freud, *The Interpretation of Dreams* (1900).

Chapter 11

1 Paper prepared by Elina Rautanen and read at the conference of the Association of British Adoption Agencies in Blackpool, December 1971.

172

Bibliography

ANSFIELD J. G., *The Adopted Child*, Springfield, Illinois: Thomas, 1971.

BERNARD V. W., 'Adoption', in Albert Deutsch and Helen Fishman (eds), *Encyclopedia of Mental Health*, Vol. 1, New York: Watts, 1963.

BOHMAN M., *Adopted Children and their Families*, Stockholm: Proprius, 1970.

BRENNER R. R., *A Follow-up Study of Adoptive Families*, New York: Child Adoption Research Committee, 1951.

CLOTHIER F., 'The psychology of the adopted child', *Mental Hygiene*, Vol. 27, 1943.

ELONEN A. S. and SCHWARTZ M. E., 'A longitudinal study of the emotional, social and academic functioning of adopted children', *Child Welfare*, Vol. 48, No. 2., 1969.

FREUD S., *The Interpretation of Dreams* (1900), trans. A. A. Brill, New York: Random House, 1938.

FREUD S., 'Family Romance', in J. Strachey (ed.) *Collected Papers*, Vol. 5, London: Hogarth Press, 1950.

GERARD M. W., *The Emotionally Disturbed Child*, New York: Child Welfare League of America, 1956.

GOODMAN J., SILBERSTEIN M. R., and MANDELL W., 'Adopted children brought to child psychiatric clinics', *Archives of General Psychiatry*, Vol. 9, 1963.

GUNTRIP H., *Schizoid Phenomena, Object Relations and the Self*, London: Hogarth Press, 1968.

Home Office, *Adoption of Children* (Houghton Committee Report, SBN 11/340356/9), HMSO, 1970.

HOOPES J. L., SHERMAN E. A., LAWDER E. A., ANDREWS R. G., and LOWER K. D., *A Follow-up Study of Adoptions* (*Vol. 2*): *Post-placement functioning of adopted children*, New York: Child Welfare League of America, 1970.

HUMPHREY M. and OUNSTED C., 'Adoptive families referred for psychiatric advice: Part I. The children', *British Journal of Psychiatry*, Vol. 109, 1963.

JAFFE B. and FANSHEL D., *How They Fared in Adoption: A follow-up study*, New York: Columbia University Press, 1970.

KIRK H. D., *Shared Fate*, New York: Free Press, 1964.

KIRK H. D., JOHASSOHN K., and FISH D. A., 'Are adopted children vulnerable to stress?', *Archives of General Psychiatry*, Vol. 14, 1966.

KOHLSAAT B. and JOHNSON M. A., 'Some suggestions for practice in infant adoption', *Social Casework*, Vol. 35, 1954.

KRUGMAN C. D., 'Differences in the relation of parents and children to adoption', *Child Welfare*, Vol. 46, No. 5, 1967.

Bibliography

LAWDER E. A., LOWER K. D., ANDREWS R. G., SHERMAN E. A., and HILL J. G., *A Follow-up Study of Adoptions Vol. 1. : Post-placement functioning of adoptive families*, New York: Child Welfare League of America, 1969.

LAWTON J. J. and GROSS Z. S., 'Review of psychiatric literature on adopted children', *Archives of General Psychiatry*, Vol. 11, 1964.

MCWHINNIE A. M., *Adopted Children: How They Grow Up*, London: Routledge & Kegan Paul, 1967.

PELLER L., 'About telling the child of his adoption', *Bulletin of the Philadelphia Association for Psycho-analysis*, Vol. 11, No. 4, 1961.

PELLER L., 'Further comments on adoption', *Bulletin of the Philadelphia Association for Psycho-analysis*, Vol. 13, No. 1, 1963.

REECE S. and LEVIN B., 'Psychiatric disturbances in adopted children: A descriptive study', *Social Work*, Vol. 13, No. 1, 1968.

SCHECHTER D. M., 'Observations on adopted children', *Archives of General Psychiatry*, Vol. 3, July 1960.

SCHECHTER D. M., CARLSON P., SIMMONS J. Q., and WORK H., 'Emotional problems in the adoptee', *Archives of General Psychiatry*, Vol. 10, 1964.

SCHWARTZ M. E., 'The family romance fantasy in children adopted in infancy', *Child Welfare*, Vol. 49, No. 7, 1970.

SIMON N. and SENTURIA A., 'Adoption and psychiatric illness', *American Journal of Psychiatry*, Vol. 122, No. 8, 1966.

TRISELIOTIS J., *Evaluation of Adoption Policy and Practice*, Edinburgh: University Department of Social Administration, 1970.

VODAK P. *et al.*, *Problems Concerning the Adoption of Children*, Prague: Czechoslovak Medical Press, 1967.

WITMER L. H., HERZOG E., WEINSTEIN E. A., and SULLIVAN M. E., *Independent Adoptions: A Follow-up Study*, New York: Russell Sage Foundation, 1963.

174

Index